Working Together:
Collaborative Information Practices for Organizational Learning

Mary M. Somerville

Association of College and Research Libraries
A division of the American Library Association
Chicago 2009

The paper used in this publication meets the minimum requirements of American National Standard for Information Sciences–Permanence of Paper for Printed Library Materials, ANSI Z39.48-1992. ∞

Library of Congress Cataloging-in-Publication Data

Somerville, Mary M.
  Working together : collaborative information practices for organizational learning / Mary M. Somerville.
    p. cm.
  Includes bibliographical references.
  ISBN 978-0-8389-8531-1 (pbk. : alk. paper) 1. Robert E. Kennedy Library--Case studies. 2. Libraries and colleges--Case studies. 3. Academic libraries--Relations with faculty and curriculum--Case studies. 4. Organizational learning--Case studies. I. Title.
  Z733.R634S66 2009
  027.7794'78--dc22
                                    2009031157
                                    2009031157

Printed in the United States of America.

13 12 11 10 09   5 4 3 2 1

Cover concept and design by Zaana Howard and Julianne Piko.

Table of Contents

Preface

Following a decade and a half of service as a university professor and nonprofit administrator, I resumed my career in library and information science in 2003. I was informed and energized during that fifteen year period by a variety of for-profit and non-profit experiences in North America, Australia, and Europe. The most compelling approaches were information-centered and learning-focused. Leaders used dialogue and reflection to foster shared understanding of organizational issues. This enabled nimble responsiveness to dynamically changing circumstances. Situational improvements occurred when an action orientation was integrated into organizational practices.

My exploration of organizational life and leadership approaches was profoundly influenced by exposure to Scandinavian style participatory action research during a Fulbright Scholar residency in 1991. As a Swedish colleague told me once about this distinctive cultural orientation: consultation and collaboration are transmitted 'through the mother's milk,' suggesting deep roots in the country's social democratic tradition of improving and understanding the world by changing it. This first-hand experience of participatory decision making and egalitarian workplace relationships inspired my subsequent eighteen year quest to create inclusive workplace learning environments in North American organizations.

My efforts were especially influenced by the applied research agenda of Dr. Anita Mirijamdotter and her colleagues at Luleå University of Technology in the north of Sweden. These social informatics professors integrated 'soft' systems thinking tools with Scandinavian design philosophies to create workplace learning experiences in 'real world' settings. Their approach derived from a qualitative research methodology developed by Dr. Peter Checkland at the University of Lancaster in the United Kingdom.

Grounded in action research and appreciative inquiry, Soft Systems Methodology convenes stakeholders, beneficiaries, and owners for purposeful dialogue. Engagement with multiple perspectives is guided by reflective 'sense making' activities which produce shared insights to guide collective action. Continuous learning occurs as participants learn their way to change, supported by enabling organizational culture and workplace practices.

My leadership toolkit was significantly enhanced in 1993 while serving as executive director of a nonprofit organization which partnered Fortune 50 corporations and higher education institutions. In this instance, my teachers were industry leaders in north Texas who promoted Dr. Peter Senge's conception of a learning organization. They understood the strategic importance of creating workplace environments that constantly enhanced workers' capabilities to create.

Toward that end, corporate executives wanted their higher education 'suppliers' to deliver graduates who were exceptionally able and engaged learners. They challenged academic institutions to improve graduates' readiness for perpetual learning within newly designed workplace environments in which expansive thinking is nurtured, collective aspirations are realized, and 'the whole' is understood.

In response, I convened conversations among presidents, provosts, deans, managers, and librarians to explore means of improving alignment between industry customer needs and academic supplier outcomes. A summer program for junior high students from underrepresented minority populations resulted. Delivered on local college campuses, the curricula prepared students to enter college science, technology, engineering, and mathematics programs. Industry mentors aided university professors in the classroom. Local schools provided bus transportation. College provosts donated instructional spaces. Continuous learning aimed at program improvement was guided by a standing committee of representatives from academe and industry. They regularly reported to the combined council of university presidents and corporate executive officers to ensure continuous alignment and sustainable funding.

When I re-entered academic librarianship, these action research insights informed my organizational leadership ambitions. The book reveals progressive insights developed over a six-year period while serving as Assistant Dean at California Polytechnic State University in San Luis Obispo, Associate Dean at San José State University, and University Librarian at the University of Colorado Denver. Initial chapters chronicle progressively collaborative design projects. Concluding chapters offer recommendations for creating learning organizations in which expansive thinking is nurtured, collective aspirations are realized, and 'the whole' is understood.

Toward this end, as I moved up the organizational career ladder, I enriched my leadership repertoire with insights from the Japanese and Australian research literatures. In particular, Dr. Christine Bruce's research reveals requisite conditions for using information as a catalyst for learning and, in the process, fostering collaboration skills and information capabilities. Professor Ikujiro Nonaka contributes a complementary design concept in proposing critical elements of an organizational learning system grounded in information exchange for knowledge creation. Like the soft systems methodology tools imported from England and the participatory design philosophy derived from Sweden, these ideas have informed workplace repurposing, reprioritizing, restructuring, and retooling—with markedly different outcomes dependent on local circumstances—in three North American libraries.

The linkage of information and learning was initially surfaced in the 1990's by Dr. Christine Bruce at Queensland University of Technology. The publication of her dissertation, *Seven Faces of Information Literacy*, provoked widespread reconsideration of information as a phenomenon. For instance, she challenged conventional skill-based notions of information literacy in proposing that individuals learn from experience with and reflection on a wide variety of information situations. Learning can therefore be seen as experiencing information usage in multiple ways. Over the past decade, Australian, Swedish, and North American researchers have extended this research through exploring how information is experienced by those who use it. In her second book, *Informed Learning*, Bruce reviews and interprets these studies, noting the small but important literature which examines workplace information competencies, developed and expressed within various professional contexts. Of particular significance, findings recently published in Australia recognize that requisite capabilities develop through workplace socialization.

The question then becomes how to design workplace environments rich in information access and exchange and fortified by dialogue and reflection opportunities. Professor Ikujiro Nonaka offers rich insights for conducting such an inquiry, based on his study of essential knowledge-enabling elements in Japanese firms. His findings underscore the importance of developing communication, decision making, and planning systems supportive of information exchange. Given that learning is social, organizations must also support the interpretative activities necessary for collective 'sense making' and idea generation.

In making a full circle to connect with its English and Swedish origins, the book's action-oriented, information-focused, and learning-centered approach advocates a participatory action orientation involving a number of disciplinary research perspectives which invite organizational participants to work together *with and for* beneficiaries to improve and understand the world by changing it.

Working Together: Information Practices for Organizational Learning describes and illustrates the efficacy of the ideas harvested from Europe, Asia, Australia, and the United States. Checkland's methodology encourages inclusive engagement in design, implementation, and evaluation activities which promote individual and collective learning. Senge's ideas on 'systems thinking' and Bruce's conception of 'informed learning' explicitly link information encounters with organizational learning. Nonaka's desire to sustain workplace inquiry promotes organizational structures and information practices. As highlights from three university libraries' experiences illustrate, these combined approaches offer rich opportunities for 'working together' to harness information in the pursuit of learning. In the process, participants at all levels of the organization are prepared to produce real world improvements amidst changing environmental circumstances.

Mary M. Somerville
November 27, 2008
Denver, Colorado

Chapter One
University Library Context

Librarians at California Polytechnic State University (Cal Poly) in San Luis Obispo were experiencing rapid technological change, aggravating financial uncertainties, and escalating community expectations. Rather than adopt the incremental approach to change which has typically characterized the profession's response to external pressures, Cal Poly librarians embarked on a journey of remarkable transformation. Willingness to embrace new ways of learning, questioning, and understanding permitted them to reconsider their roles and responsibilities in the light of changing perceptions about their users and their work. In the process, they transformed the organization and re-invented their purpose.

The goal throughout this three year journey was to better align the Library with university learning, teaching, and research priorities. With this intention, professional and paraprofessional staff members initiated several action research studies, conducted from 2003 to 2006, which gave 'authentic voice' to student and faculty constituencies. Profound changes occurred: reference desk service and 'stand alone' instruction formerly comprising librarians' exclusive attention was replaced by collaborative work focused on research portal development, course integrated instruction, 'learning collection' development, and specialized research consultation. In this new learning community, librarians pro-actively exchanged insights with learning partners comprised of a growing circle of campus stakeholders. They abandoned 'information hoarding' and 'organizational silos' in favor of information exchange and sense making activities within a vibrant community-of-practice. Moving beyond individualistic behaviors and attitudes, they adopted an inquiry orientation conducive to collective exploration and experimentation.

These organizational changes served to prepare librarians to work together in new ways and, as well, to renegotiate relationships with paraprofessional colleagues. Well aligned with professional trends to move beyond 'sitting at the reference desk', tending infrequently consulted reference books, and counting 'sage on the stage' bibliographic instruction sessions, this workplace transformation initiative also prepared long time reference librarians to repurpose their expertise. They learned to reinvent library services, systems, and programs 'for and with users' and other learning partner 'stakeholders'. Concurrently, library leaders learned to recognize that nimble organizational responsiveness depends on collaborative information practices fostered by workplace reflection and dialogue.

This book chronicles the journey. It conveys how employees learned to trust themselves, each other, and their constituencies. Case studies demonstrate that management learned to trust the staff to manage and lead change. And practical examples illustrate the characteristics of organizational development tools that can produce transformative and sustainable workplace learning.

Changing Organizational Patterns

At Cal Poly, for as long as anyone could remember, librarians 'sat at the desk.' For at least two decades, this occupational habit was supplemented by didactic teaching, in which students sat passively as librarians lectured about library research mechanics. Reference transactions and instructional sessions were routinely counted and reported to library administrators. However, no use was made of these numbers. Nor was assessment of either reference services or instructional services conducted. Rather, relevancy was assumed, because 'it's always been that way.'

Similarly, annual staff performance reviews were largely anecdotal in nature, permitting employees to continue doing what they had always done, undeterred by evaluation criteria. Organizational funding for travel and training was likewise assumed to benefit individual employees, with no expectation that personal enrichment would benefit co-workers. Although there was some seasonal variation in the pace of activities that would at times enliven the building, for the most part a pervasive malaise characterized the workplace. Within this staid environment, periodic announcements of 'another budget cut' or an 'unfunded mandate' interrupted workplace calm. Over time, financial erosion left management with few alternatives but to convert retirements into permanent salary savings through eliminating positions that, if filled, would jeopardize the library acquisition budget.

This was the situation presented to me when I interviewed for the position of Assistant Dean of Information, Instruction, and Research Services. So when I was confronted with a permanent ten percent reduction in the annual base budget soon after I commenced employment, I accelerated our consideration of organizational priorities. Legacy programs such as the reference desk and learning resources center earned particularly thorough examination because their personnel salaries accounted for twenty five percent of the library's annual budget.

These program reviews produced unexpected revelations. We discovered that most directional questions could be adequately addressed by improved signage. The majority of technology related questions could be solved by enforcing existing service agreements for regular machine maintenance. Few research queries were presented which required specialized professional reference expertise. The remaining informational questions were characteristically low-level and assignment based.

Similarly, review of the learning resources center revealed that over time this model 'library within a library', begun two decades earlier to serve the teacher education program, no longer satisfied state and national standards. Both the curriculum collection and the service model were woefully out of date. In combination with the budget crisis, this evidence permitted—and, in fact, required—radical reconsideration of organizational priorities and resource allocations.

Early Re-Design Activities

In many libraries, this crisis would not have precipitated an organizational journey down a path of fundamental change. Librarians would instead have 'tightened their belt' once again. In our case, however, librarians recognized that we had reached a point where we could no longer 'do more with less'. They were therefore willing to reconsider fundamental workplace assumptions. As they reconsidered, they came to understand the need to engage in a deeper effort to repurpose and retool. This required a change in how they thought and what they thought about as they 'learned their way to change'. In addition, these information professionals began to use the abundant data that the organization had been collecting but not analyzing or interpreting.

Over time, the situation changed as data was regularly converted into information which supported collective decision making. As a result of these findings, librarians were replaced at the reference desk by paraprofessionals in public and technical services. Former reference librarians then applied their subject expertise to create disciplinary content for digital research portals seamlessly integrated into course curricula. Librarians also assumed collection development duties well beyond the traditional tending of print reference tools. Their responsibilities soon encompassed evaluation and development of all print and electronic collections, including electronic resources management systems. It quite naturally followed that traditional boundaries between technical and public services blurred through active collaboration to advance digital migration and improve customer service.

Annual professional development plans with explicit learning goals became a means for former reference librarians to guide themselves to re-invention. Measurable outcomes aligned with both university and library strategic plans detailed their progressive evolution into subject specialists with strong academic department affiliations (Davis & Somerville 2006). Collective learning was ensured through regular information exchange opportunities at weekly meetings formerly consumed by 'housekeeping details.'

Paraprofessionals from the decommissioned learning resources center were also prepared for new responsibilities in information and reference services (Somerville, Huston, & Mirijamdotter 2005; Somerville, Schader, & Huston 2005). They were soon joined by technical services volunteers. Librarians supported staff success by delivering weekly sessions offering solutions to difficult reference questions and tactics for successful online database searches. This educational series built paraprofessionals' expertise incrementally over time. It also familiarized staff with librarians' expertise so they could make appropriate referrals for users with specialized research queries.

Initially the training content was librarian-driven. Staff soon learned, however, to anticipate their collective learning needs. They assumed responsibility for developing their own meeting agendas, including scheduling subject specialists' presentations. In addition, as their learning expectations matured, staff members requested 'hands on' learning experiences rather than a traditional style lecture. They also requested development of a database system into which librarians deposited course assignments. Enriched with annotations detailing step by step directions for assisting students, this 'boundary crossing' knowledge base served to advance both student and paraprofessional research competence.

The newly created assignment database was soon complemented by a blog-based forum that enabled staff to work together on solutions (Somerville & Vazquez 2004). Suggestive of their growing efficacy, paraprofessionals named this system RISE—which mirrored enthusiasm for new responsibilities for research and instruction services and education. It also reflected their emerging appreciation for the considerable knowledge of paraprofessional colleagues with advanced educational degrees and rich workplace experiences.

As paraprofessionals were engaged with increasingly important relationships and responsibilities, the 'first contact' staffing model freed public services librarians to develop relationships outside the library with campus constituencies. New professional priorities emerged which emphasized specialized research consultation, digital learning initiatives (e.g., Somerville & Vuotto, 2005; Somerville, Rogers, Mirijamdotter, & Partridge 2007), and information-centered instruction (e.g., Elrod & Somerville 2007).

Collaborative Design Fundamentals

Through working together in new ways, professionals and paraprofessionals reinvented the library's research, information, and instruction programs. An action research orientation ensured real world improvements, including new campus outreach roles for librarians. Librarians next elected to expand their scope of influence and involvement by inviting student generated research, initiating curriculum integration, and encouraging facilities experimentation.

References

Davis, H. L., & Somerville, M. M. (2006). Learning our way to change: Improved institutional alignment. *New Library World, 107*(3/4), 127–140.

Elrod, S., & Somerville, M. M. (2007). Literature based scientific learning: A collaboration model. *Journal of Academic Librarianship, 33*(6), 684–691.

Somerville, M. M., Huston, M. E., & Mirijamdotter, A. (2005). Building on what we know: Staff development in the digital age. *The Electronic Library, 23*(4), 480–491.

Somerville, M. M., Rogers, E., Mirijamdotter, A., & Partridge, H. (2007). Collaborative evidence-based information practice: The Cal Poly digital learning initiative. In E. Connor (Ed.), *Evidence-Based Librarianship: Case Studies and Active Learning Exercises* (pp. 141–161). Oxford, England: Chandos Publishing.

Somerville, M. M., Schader, B., & Huston, M. E. (2005). Rethinking what we do and how we do it: Systems thinking strategies for library leadership. *Australian Academic and Research Libraries, 36*(4), 214–227.

Somerville, M. M., & Vazquez, F. (2004). Constructivist workplace learning: An idealized design project. In P. A. Danaher, C. Macpherson, F. Nouwens, & D. Orr (Eds.), *Proceedings of the 3rd International Lifelong Learning Conference*, Yeppoon, Queensland, Australia, (pp. 300–305 plus errata page). Rockhampton, Australia: Central Queensland University.

Somerville, M. M., & Vuotto, F. (2005). If you build it with them, they will come: Digital research portal design and development strategies. *Internet Reference Services Quarterly: A Journal of Innovative Information Practice, Technologies, and Resources, 10*(1), 77–94.

Chapter Two
Student Co-Design Projects

The times are fraught with dynamic, converging forces that challenge libraries' traditional roles of building resource collections, facilitating document access, and enabling intellectual attribution. Most prominently, the first years of the new millennium have seen dramatic changes in how information is produced, as well as how it is accessed, organized, and communicated (e.g., Fallows 2008; OCLC 2002, 2003, 2005).

For example, individuals can now produce and share their own information, rather than waiting for book or journal publishers to create and deliver the material—a concept known as peer production. Internet-based social networking sites offer yet another popular way to create and exchange unmediated information. Because these new technology tools enable easy information production and consumption, individuals increasingly circumvent what has traditionally been the role of libraries—organizing, managing, and accessing information.

Furthermore, most North American students have grown up with the digital technologies developed in the last decades of the 20th century and now widely available in the new millennium. These students have spent their entire lives using computers, video games, digital music players, video cameras, mobile phones, e-mail, instant messaging, and other technology tools and toys. As a result, these 'digital natives' (Prensky 2005, 2007) think and act differently (Windham 2005, 2006) than the people for whom higher education—and academic libraries—were historically designed to serve (Lippincott 2005, Brown & Adler 2008, Gibbons 2007, Foster & Gibbons 2008).

As technologies have transformed how information is experienced, even the commonly held conception of information has changed. Today information is seen as something with which—and around which—people interact (Milne 2007), rendering mere content delivery inadequate. Consequently, as new technology tools enable effortless information consumption and peer knowledge production, libraries are forced to reconsider professional purposes, responsibilities, and relationships (Somerville & Brar 2007).

Initial User Study

In recognition of this changing environment, librarians at California Polytechnic State University (Cal Poly) initiated a process to find out more about present and potential users' needs and preferences. To explore students' points of view, librarians initially adapted a qualitative research approach used by Dr. Christine Bruce (1997) to investigate information literacy conceptions among Australian higher educators. She discovered that learning is about changes in conception, learning always has content as well as process, learning is about relations between the learner and the subject matter, and improving learning requires understanding learners' perspectives (Bruce 2008). Intrigued by the connection between information and learning, the librarians adapted Bruce's questions to explore the differing ways in which Cal Poly students experience, perceive, understand, and conceptualize information conceptions and information usage. They planned to use the research findings to initiate exploratory conversations with campus faculty and students.

A graduate student in library science conducted open-ended interviews to explore nineteen college students' information conceptions and information usage. He asked student subjects: "How do you use information to complete class assignments?" "How do you use information outside of your coursework?" "Tell a story of a time when you used information well." "Describe your view of someone who used information well." "Describe your experience using information." Neutral verbal prompts encouraged students to elaborate.

After interview sessions were completed, staff members transcribed audio recordings to permit assignment of 'emergent categories' describing students' varying ways of experiencing information usage and its advancement. Transcription analysis revealed three primary ways in which undergraduate students conceptualize information and its usage: 'sources'—in which information use is seen as finding information located in information sources; 'processes'—in which information use is seen as initiating a process; and 'purposes'—in which information use is seen as building a personal knowledge base for various purposes (Maybee 2006).

Students who experienced the 'sources' aspect of information encounters focused on knowledge sources and their characteristics, whether print, electronic, or human. They believed that knowledge of sources—including organizational schema—enabled successful retrieval of the ideas contained within them. As a junior level architecture student stated about her recent research paper experience, "I used a lot of different sources of information, not just the Internet, which is not always reliable." A senior computer science student echoed this sentiment when she said, "It depends on what sites you go to, but I do not think you can be as trusting on the Internet as you can be with a book that has been published and theoretically edited."

In further describing source characteristics, a junior engineering student noted about book indices, "I definitely think that the amount of information you get from something like that depends a lot on just how that book is organized and indexed, because most of the books will not have very much information on the specific topic that you are trying to research. They'll have bits and pieces throughout the book so the better the index, the better you can locate the information that you need". He next compared book indexes to electronic search tools, saying, "On the Web, it is a lot easier because you can use search engines to find exactly what you want. And if you have a large document, you can use key words to locate the types of information that you specifically want, so you know what to read." In focusing on the sources conception of information usage, subjects concentrated on information finding. Information is viewed objectively, separate and distinct from the student subject. And information use is a secondary concern, which occurred after information acquisition.

Students holding a 'process' orientation conceptualized information use as initiating and facilitating a process which began with recognizing an information need. As a junior engineering student stated, "I go off-roading a lot and I wanted to upgrade some of the parts on my truck. So in this case, I wanted to buy a new rear-end for the truck and upgrade to a stronger one." Following recognition of the information need, he conducted an information search involving a variety of strategies, which emerged during the course of the investigation. "I consulted the vehicle manual of the truck that I own, talked to people on message boards, talked to people who knew a lot more than I did about vehicles and about axles and found out what I needed to look for. Once I had established the specifications of what I was looking for, I took those specifications and started looking for the rear-end that I wanted. In junkyards, I could not find what I wanted. Then I found a Web site which specialized in that type of thing where you can post classifieds."

In illustrating the application of a 'process' approach to academic studies, a junior business administration student described how he refined his search strategy. His words convey a sense of the importance of information evaluation: "Usually more information is better, but if the information is incorrect, obviously that's not going to help. If it's biased or not objective, then it's not going to be helpful. If it's not relevant, that's not helpful. So, better than lots of information—I feel that I get lots of information but it's not really the information that relates to what I'm thinking about at that time—in life, pertinent information that relates to the very reason for your search is more helpful." As with the sources conception, information is viewed as separate and distinct from the user. Instead, the primary focus is the processes used to obtain information. Although information is part of the process described by subjects, information must be obtained before it can be used.

The third category of participants conceptualized information use as building a knowledge base which could then be used for a variety of 'purposes'. These subjects focused on the ways in which they use information. Information usages included decision making and problem solving, forming a personal and disciplinary point-of-view, and formally and informally exchanging information. A junior level psychology student described her knowledge base usage in these terms: "I think there is a vast body of information and knowledge that you just gather as you grow up. Those are just some of the resources of information I use." Another student, a junior male political science student, explained how information obtained in one course applies to other endeavors: "It is my view that whenever you do an assignment like that, it sticks with you. I then can adapt that into whatever part of my life I'm in, such as conversations, social interaction, and issues that may come up in the future outside of education. Who knows, maybe a year down the road an issue will come up outside the sphere of education and that information that I pursued to do that assignment will be relevant."

These subjects reflected a concern not present among subjects expressing either a source or process focus: students with a purpose orientation acknowledged the importance of understand the viewpoints of information providers, rather than the need to evaluate the credibility of the information. As a sophomore graphic design student described her information encounters, "So, you'll receive it, take it for what it's worth, but then kind of form your own opinion about it. You don't just take it and believe it. I mean sometimes we do, but you always have to analyze it on your own." In its maturity, a purpose orientation produces someone who uses information well, as expressed in the words of this junior political science student, "Basically, if they understand the information they are gathering, such as if they understand the different laws as pertaining to doing business, then they will be able to do business much more effectively than if they just went out there willy-nilly and said, 'I want to do it so I'm just going to do it. I don't really understand what things are regulating this, but I guess if I find out I'll know then.' This is a very dangerous route to travel. In that respect, the use of information would be very important." Another sophomore animal science student described the importance of synthesizing learning outcomes from course assignments. She said, "If I can take some sort of information that either has been presented to me or that I have gone and found and I can take that and apply it—like use it and understand it deeply enough to apply it—then that is pretty much as far as you can get with anything." As these interview excerpts illustrate, the primary focus of this awareness structure is on how information is used. Therefore, a purposeful intention drives an application orientation which, secondarily, builds a knowledge base. In marked contrast to the sources and processes conceptions formerly described, students with a purpose conception view information subjectively. In this conception, information is an integral part of the individual.

The Cal Poly research results support the findings of other phenomenographic researchers in Australia (Lupton 2004, 2008), Sweden (Limberg & Folkesson 2006), the United Kingdom (Webber, Boon, & Johnston 2005), and the United States (Feind 2008) who recommend providing students with learning activities that simultaneously activate and extend prior information use experiences. It follows that, within an academic setting, students are most successful when instructional activities are situated within an evolving disciplinary context providing multi-faceted and multi-tiered learning opportunities. This insight galvanized librarians' intention to re-consider the Library's 'librarian-centric' instructional assumptions.

This commitment emerged quite naturally, as 'making sense' of the interview data together interrupted librarians' 'unceasing doing' and, in its place, encouraged dialogue and reflection. These inquiring conversations ignited more questions about students' information finding and using proficiencies and preferences. In turn, this fueled the need to understand how to become more successful enablers of experiential student learning and more responsive designers of information discovery pathways.

Achievement of this twofold aspiration required that librarians better understand how students (and other present and potential users) experience information. In addition, it required heightened appreciation for the depth and breadth of students' previous information experiences. As the study results illustrate, students are not 'information illiterate' when they enter college. Rather, they possess significant experiential knowledge from having successfully negotiated other information rich situations prior to entering academe. This insight crystallized an organizational commitment to collaboratively inquire with users on (re) design and, ultimately, (re)invention of library systems, services, and programs. The distinctive campus educational philosophy—'learn by doing'—shaped the process for realizing these organizational goals.

'Learn by Doing' Tenets

The 'learn by doing' educational tradition—within which Cal Poly librarians practiced—recognized that learning involves process as well as content. This is in keeping with contemporary learning theory across a wide range of disciplines, including library and information science (e.g., Kuhlthau 2003). Within the Cal Poly culture, this meant that faculty supervisors were encouraged to provide students with real world learning experiences. Therefore, librarians recognized that they could better understand students' information finding and using activities by more deeply embedding themselves into course learning activities. In the process, they also intended to increase their conversance with faculty members' course content and learning outcomes.

Librarians initially decided to invite computer science professors to supervise student research projects which focused on library relevant topics because information services and systems are increasingly technology-enabled. They negotiated course assignment requirements so that students assumed responsibility for problem definition, methodological implementation, and data analysis. This proved to be a fortuitous decision: from 2004 to 2006, reliance on student-framed, student-conducted, and student-reported research results produced rich evidence about different types of students, their information use at various stages—and why this is so, and their learning style and media delivery preferences.

In so doing, librarians evolved a unique, but transferable, collaborative research approach which involved students in a range of learning activities that improved electronic search tools, enhanced library website functionalities, and enabled multimedia 'knowledge making' projects. Project outcomes included co-created digital learning objects, digital learning activities, and digital learning environments.

This collaborative design ('co-design') approach is highly participatory in nature. It benefits from the knowledge of students who have grown up with digital technologies. As a result, these digital natives think and act differently than the people for whom today's libraries were designed. Consequently, librarians reasoned, organizational services and systems must change accordingly, 'with and for' users.

The examples which follow are meant to illustrate the potential of 'learning to learn' with users. In so doing, librarians relinquished the pervasive professional assumption that 'we know what they need.' In the process, librarians changed how they thought and what they thought about. As later chapters illustrate, this insight also transformed how librarians forged learning partnerships with other campus stakeholders.

Search Interface Re-Design

Third year computer science students enrolled in a human-computer interaction course were invited to evaluate an 'out of the box' federated search engine produced by a commercial vendor. It was designed to simultaneously interrogate multiple proprietary databases. Project parameters assumed that a user interface—the means by which end users communicate with technology or technology systems—required careful consideration of the context of usage. Therefore, students were asked to mediate between the world(s) of end users (their student peers) and the world of technology in order to bring the two together in an ultimately productive relationship.

The research project explored problems with the search system interface which were of significant concern to students. In the initial study, the student research teams focused on various aspects of the question: "How can we improve the 'out of the box' interface to an electronic meta-database retrieval system providing federated search engine access to the library's expensive online databases of scholarly journals, newspapers, and other research resources?" The supervising computer science professor proposed that team members develop an interface design that would be usable and efficient for both students and faculty. In addition, students aimed to design overall branding for the site so users would be able to easily distinguish library owned or subscribed content through distinctive color schemes and graphic elements.

In their initial investigations, student researchers selected a variety of user-centered design approaches to seek input from their peers. For instance, they developed, tested, and implemented a questionnaire that focused on student research habits, student research skills, and student learning styles. In addition, they conducted usability studies on the 'out of the box' interface. These insights were supplemented by peer-to-peer interviews and student-led focus groups. Throughout, student researchers and student subjects were as representative as possible of the university's undergraduate population.

In the second stage, student teams compared single databases' 'native' interface functionalities with the commercial federated product. This comparison yielded a list of customization recommendations. Then they tested the efficacy of their recommendations by asking their peers to complete four task scenarios using both the original release of the commercial interface and 'paper prototypes' reflecting interface customization. These activities revealed additional design problems.

These efforts informed the evolution of a series of prototypes, ranging from chalkboard mock-ups to high-fidelity final products. The prototypes addressed all facets of the commercial product interface, including screen designs, navigation tabs, icons, logos and buttons. Research findings were submitted to librarians regularly throughout the quarter to encourage two-way dialogue that advanced both student and librarian learning.

In the final report, students recommended that the federated search interface should mirror the 'look and feel' of Google. It should also provide a customizable personal information environment, a 'my space'. A 'my e-shelf' would support organization of citations and a document archive would house peer-reviewed papers. A 'my databases' function would capture search histories, supplemented by current alert services. Students also recommended various means of branding the user search experience to signal to users that retrieval outcomes were library hosted.

Librarians considered the results so useful that, after the digital services staff had implemented the students' recommendations in a local release, they forwarded the students' report to the product vendor. The vendor was also excited about the students' recommendations and implemented many of the features and functions in the next product release.

This collaborative research experience also served to introduce librarians to interface design, moving them from their traditional passive stance as consumers of commercial database products to co-designers of user-centered interfaces which enable information interaction and knowledge creation. The fledgling research partnership also furthered librarians' commitment to collaborative user-centered information practices.

In this initial collaborative design experience, librarians learned to examine the underlying assumptions and beliefs that traditionally guided their workplace decision making. They recognized that achievement of user-guided thinking requires reconsidering traditional assumptions about what to study, as well as how—and with whom—to consult. And they gained insight into the knowledge creation potential of working in new ways with beneficiaries—in this case, students and faculty—to repurpose, retool, and reprioritize their professional expertise.

Learning Environment Design

A second project involved senior students in a human computer interaction course on user-centered content architecture design. Students initiated their investigation by asking: "What do faculty and students know about library resources? What do they want to know? And how do they want to learn it?" Initial research results revealed that the overwhelming majority of both faculty and students did not know what a librarian did or how to find one. In addition, when students were asked where they conducted research, seventy-two percent replied that they used the Internet. Only four percent said that they went to the library. Although most students reported using the library website occasionally, an overwhelming majority expressed surprise in hearing that library services offered assistance in finding books, journals and other academic resources. Instead, students relied on assistance from friends within their social network

After analyzing this data, student researchers recommended to librarians that, given undergraduates' online focus, the library should enhance its presence on the Internet. Students suggested that librarians co-create digital learning environments, such as disciplinary research portals that apply proven interaction design principles. This suggestion initiated new roles for librarians as content providers for web based learning environments.

Students' notions about content design acknowledged the 'dimensionality' of the target audience, including academic level considerations and other user attributes which produce different needs at various stages in students' careers. These researchers also recommended that viewing experiences accommodate learning style differences. They sought to resolve the differences between systems' traditional patterns of information provision and users' natural processes of information use. Toward that end, team members proposed a research portal content architecture that mapped information elements to web page components. Following this, they implemented a usability study to inform minor improvements in navigation and layout.

Based on these results, student researchers hypothesized that implementation of a 'scaffolded' approach would assist students to move from one level of learning to the next as their academic career evolved. They sought to appropriately bridge the gap between their peers' actual knowledge and potential development through presentation of appropriately difficult challenges and accompanying support. Toward that end, students developed a two-dimensional (2-D) content architecture for a disciplinary research portal. See Table 1.

The design concept recognized user attribute 'dimensionality', which produces different needs at various stages in students' careers. It also acknowledged that viewing experiences should accommodate learning style differences.

Table 1. Content Architecture Model Excerpt (adapted from Somerville, et al., 2007)

	Lower Years (first two of four year program)	Intermediate Year (third)	Advanced Year (fourth)
Visual and Kinesthetic	More research content breadth but less in depth and basic research strategies needed, paired with visual and kinesthetic presentation elements—e.g., use graphics and demonstrations and replace textual information with visual representations (graphs or diagrams)	Discipline-based coursework and higher order thinking experiences require more in depth information resources and research strategies, with continued application of visual and kinesthetic design elements	More in depth topical content, presented within disciplinary framework, to enable more ambitious research purposes, with consistent application of visual and kinesthetic design elements
Auditory and Read/Write	More research content breadth but less in depth and basic research strategies needed, paired with audio and read-write presentation elements—e.g., re-organize diagram or graph content into statements and offer both textual narrative and audio recordings, such as podcasts	Discipline-based coursework and higher order thinking experiences require more in depth information resources and research strategies, with continued application of audio and read-write elements	More in depth topical content, presented within disciplinary framework, to enable more ambitious research purposes, with consistent application of audio and read-write elements

Collaborative Design Elements

In the Library co-design projects, students were invited to generate research questions, select research methodologies, and interpret research data for presentation to librarians. They employed a variety of interactive and user-centric research methods, with supervision from faculty sponsors. Throughout, librarians provided coaching services upon request, explaining information searching, evaluation, and dissemination strategies through their professional bibliographic lens. In turn, they learned from students about non-bibliographically controlled sources of authoritative information and, as well, social networking and peer knowledge production practices and technologies.

Such collaborative design activities offer a number of important benefits. First, data collection and interpretation require considerable face-to-face communication between librarians and students. This clarifying dialogue offers librarians valuable insights into user perspectives and fulfills contemporary expectations for substantial engagement around information. In addition, when librarians' relationships with students continue beyond the semester, ongoing communication enriches mutual appreciation of a wide range of library issues and opportunities. This collaborative approach naturally encourages continuous organizational improvements, even as it fosters sustainable learning relationships with members of diverse campus communities. And, finally, ongoing conversations continue library wide rethinking and re-orientation which improves the library's contributions to the university's learning, teaching, and research priorities.

This approach reflects a fundamental shift in higher education from an emphasis on teaching to a focus on learning. Reliance on student-generated evidence also acknowledges that today's generation of students are able information consumers, as well as confident knowledge producers. Student-centered learning, therefore, requires reconsideration of traditional non-consultative approaches to education delivery. These converging factors compelled librarians to move from 'library-centric' to 'user-centered' decision making processes, which involved—and, in fact, required—continued learning 'with and from' student and faculty learning partners.

References

Brown, J. S., & Adler, R. P. (2008). Minds on fire: Open education, the long tail, and Learning 2.0. *EDUCAUSE Review*, 43(1), 16–32. Available: http://www.johnseelybrown.com/mindsonfire.pdf

Bruce, C. (1997). *The seven faces of information literacy*. Adelaide, Australia: Auslib Press. For a summary, see: http://sky.fit.qut.edu.au/~bruce/inflit/faces/faces1.php

Bruce, C. S. (2008). *Informed learning*. Chicago: Association of College and Research Libraries.

Fallows, D. (2008). *Search engine use*, Pew Internet & American Life Project, Washington D.C. Available: http://www.pewinternet.org/pdfs/PIP_Search_Aug08.pdf

Feind, R. (2008). Results of a phenomenographic investigation of how faculty and staff perceive, engage in, and view information literacy. *The International Journal of Learning* 14(12), 167–170.

Foster, N. F., & Gibbons, S. (2008). *Studying students: The undergraduate research project at the University of Rochester*. Chicago: Association of College & Research Libraries.

Gibbons, S. (2007). *The academic library and the NextGen student*. Chicago: ALA Editions.

Kuhlthau, C. C. (2003). *Seeking meaning: A process approach to library and information services*. 2nd ed.

Limberg, L., & Folkesson, L. (2006). Information seeking, didactics and learning (IDOL). Summary in English. In Undervisning i informationssökning. Slutrapport från projektet Informationssökning, didaktik och lärande (IDOL). [Teaching information seeking. Final report from the project Information seeking, didactics and learning.] (pp. 8–10). Borås, Sweden: Valfrid.

Lippincott, J. K. (2005). Net Generation students and libraries. In D. G. Oblinger & J. L. Oblinger (Eds). *Educating the Net Generation, EDUCAUSE*, Boulder, Colorado, pp. 13.1–13.15. Available: http://www.educause.edu/EducatingtheNetGeneration/5989

Lupton, M. (2004). *The learning connection: information literacy and the student experience*. Auslib Press, Adelaide.

Lupton, M. (2008). *Information literacy and learning*. Ph.D. dissertation, Queensland University of Technology, Australia. Available: http://adt.library.qut.au

Maybee, C. (2006). Undergraduate perceptions of information use: The basis for creating user-centered student information literacy instruction. *Journal of Academic Librarianship*, 32(1), 79–85.

Milne, A. (2007). Entering the Interaction Age: implementing a future vision for campus learning spaces … today. EDUCAUSE Review, 42(1), 12–31. Available: http://connect.educause.edu/Library/EDUCAUSE+Review/EnteringtheInteractionAge/40680

OCLC Online Computer Library Center, Inc. (2002), *OCLC White paper on the information habits of college students*, OCLC, Dublin, Ohio. Available: http://www.oclc.org/research/announcements/2002-06-24.htm

OCLC Online Computer Library Center, Inc. (2003), A. Wilson, ed., *The 2003 OCLC Environmental Scan: Pattern Recognition*, Dublin, Ohio. Available: http://www.oclc.org/reports/escan/toc.htm

OCLC Online Computer Library Center, Inc. (2005), *Perceptions of Libraries and Information Resources*, OCLC, Dublin, Ohio. Available: http://www.oclc.org/reports/2005perceptions.htm

Prensky, M. (2005). Engage me or enrage me: what today's learners demand. *EDUCAUSE Review*, 40(5), 60–65. Available: http://www.educause.edu/ir/library/pdf/ERM0553.pdf

Prensky, M. (2007). To educate, we must listen: reflections from traveling the world. Available: http://www.marcprensky.com/writing/Prensky-To_Educate,We_Must_Listen.pdf

Somerville, M. M., & Brar, N. (2007). Toward co-creation of knowledge in the Interaction Age: An organizational case study. In H. K. Kaul & S. Kaul (Eds.), *Papers of the Tenth National Convention on Knowledge, Library and Information Networking (NACLIN 2007)*, (pp. 367–376). New Delhi, India: Developing Library Network.

Somerville, M. M., Rogers, E., Mirijamdotter, A., & Partridge, H. (2007). Collaborative evidence-based information practice: The Cal Poly digital learning initiative. In E. Connor (Ed.), *Evidence-Based Librarianship: Case Studies and Active Learning Exercises* (pp. 141–161). Oxford, England: Chandos Publishing.

Webber, Sheila, Stuart Boon, & Bill Johnston. (2005). A comparison of UK academics' conceptions of information literacy in two disciplines: English and Marketing." *Library & Information Research*, 29, (93): 4–15.

Windham, C. (2005). Father Google and Mother IM: Confessions of a Net Gen Learner, *EDUCAUSE Review* (September/October), 43–58.

Windham, C. (2006). Getting Past Google: Perspectives on Information Literacy from the Millennial Mind, in D. Oblinger (ed.) *EDUCAUSE Learning Initiative (ELI)*, September, Paper 3, 10 pp. Available at: http://www.educause.edu/ir/library/pdf/ELI3007.pdf

Chapter Three
Faculty Co-Design Partnership

Library reference transactions steadily decline while Internet traffic soars. The predominance of e-resources transforms information search patterns, processes, and preferences. Increasingly, users demand 'anytime, anyplace' search systems, digital resources, and research consultation. And, amidst these dynamically changing circumstances, higher educators and academic librarians recognize the necessity of replacing traditional instructional methods with more student-centered learning experiences (Somerville & Brar 2009).

Within that context, a California Polytechnic State University librarian partnered with business faculty to advance student learning. They aimed to further relationships among individuals and ideas through enriched information encounters that harnessed the information and communication technologies precipitating this revolution.

Collaborative Learning Partnership

This faculty-librarian partnership was all the more remarkable because it was initiated by business professors. They recognized that students were overwhelmed by the vast array of print and electronic information resources. To address this situation, they recognized the need to involve the business librarian in a curriculum revision initiative initiated in 2004.

Discussions were initially wide ranging. For instance, undergraduate case study assignments were considered in the light of frequently asked business reference questions. Industry trends and employer expectations were compared to the department's graduation requirements. 'Gaps' prompted consideration of new approaches to prepare students for both academic and workplace success since, all agreed, simply adding more content to the curriculum was neither feasible nor effective.

Dialogue next turned to exploration of curriculum-driven information literacy approaches which would both guide students through the labyrinth of disciplinary research tools and resources and also develop capabilities transferable to successfully navigating a myriad of other information intensive situations. The original thinking was that a business information literacy web site would complement the business librarian's in-person classroom presentations on business research tools and search strategies. During the course of the project, however, considerable value was added to the portal concept so that information resources and information literacy could be fully integrated into curricular teaching and learning activities (Vuotto 2004). The librarian was

19

then relieved of the obligation to deliver 'one shot' 50-minute instructional sessions. Instead, because the portal delivered disciplinary research essentials, he could pursue other learning enrichment activities.

The digital research portal project aimed to advance students' information proficiencies and, concurrently, their disciplinary mastery. These learning assumptions recognized that "information literacy is necessarily demonstrated in a context and within a domain of content" (Catts 2004, 2) encompassing "an intellectual framework for recognizing the need for understanding, finding, evaluating, and using information. These are activities which may be supported in part by fluency with information technology, in part by sound investigatory methods, but most importantly throughout critical discernment and reasoning" (Lupton 2004, 4).

Better integration of information literacy and information resources into the curriculum depended on heightening the robust learning partnership between the business librarian and business faculty. This evolved out of their shared understanding that learning involves changes in conceptions, as expressed through the relationships between the learner and the subject matter, as captured by the concept of 'relational' information literacy (Bruce 1997).

Throughout this evolving learning partnership, the business librarian used his professional understanding of knowledge generating practices and disciplinary information structures to surface essential elements for advancing students' situated understanding, finding, evaluating, and using of information. Working together, the business faculty and the librarian sought to advance students' investigatory methods, as well as their critical discernment and reasoning, within the context of disciplinary knowledge.

These notions about disciplinary research proficiencies conveniently coincided with faculty members' convictions about business graduates' requisite skills. Professors recognized that technology and communication advances have transformed the world into a global community, with colleagues and competitors as likely to live and work in India as in Indianapolis (Partnership for 21st Century Skills 2003). Moreover, within contemporary workplace decision-making environments, flattened hierarchies require employees to both work productively in teams and also communicate successfully with customers. Given these realities, employers now require that entry-level employees are prepared to acquire new knowledge, learn new technologies, process information rapidly, make informed decisions, and communicate information influentially.

Disciplinary Knowledge Fundamentals

In preplanning discussions, project planners adopted the 'relational' information literacy framework advanced by the Australian and New Zealand Institute for

Information Literacy and the Council of Australian University Librarians (2004). These bodies suggest that well prepared graduates are capable of abstract thinking about information and its manipulation. This implies that students become conversant with major disciplinary resources in their field of study. Graduates are able to frame researchable questions as well as to locate, evaluate, manage, and use information in a range of contexts and a variety of media. Finally, they can interpret and present information in a variety of forms—written, statistical, graphs, charts, diagrams, and tables.

Portal content scope and outcomes were formulated through explicit discussion about how information comes to be created, discovered, analyzed, and evaluated in the field of business. This 'meta' gaze served to explore 'information about information' (Lant 2001). A series of information-centered questions informed dialogue about the knowledge, research, questions, studies, and activities most appropriate to advancing essential disciplinary learning outcomes. This line of inquiry also served to define portal content scope and structure by considering such discipline-specific questions as:

- From what other fields did this field of study derive its origins? At what point was this field recognized?
- Has the collection, analysis, evaluation, or presentation of information changed over the years since the inception of this field of study?

This context setting dialogue naturally led to exploring the field's information structure in more detail. In doing so, faculty members were guided by librarians' curiosity about 'information about information', including:

- What constitutes information in this field? Since the field's inception, how has the definition of appropriate information changed? Have certain sources of information fallen out of favor or become more reputable with the passage of time?
- Does this field of study involve different levels of information—for instance, primary, secondary, data, and/or metadata?
- Where does information in this field come from? How is it collected? Who collects it? Who comments upon it?
- How is information stored? Where is information archived?
- In what format is information in this field presented? In what form is commentary upon information presented?
- Is information in the field presented numerically, textually, visually? Which media are most important in the storage and presentation of information in this field?

The intense scrutiny devoted to explicating aspects of the discipline's information environment reflected shared conviction that disciplinary mastery evolves as students develop increasingly more sophisticated understanding of information sources, information use, and information management. This line of inquiry led quite easily to considering how well contextualized information encounters could cultivate these higher level thinking capabilities—within the broader context of the marketing department curriculum. For this purpose, other guiding questions proved useful:

- What constitutes relevant research in the field? How does one frame a relevant question?
- How does a researcher access information needed to answer questions effectively and efficiently?
- How and where is disciplinary information stored? Who determines which information will be stored?
- Are special skills needed to discover information in the field? If yes, what are those skills?
- Are there restrictions on who can collect information? Are legal or ethical issues involved in its collection?

Following this discussion of research, discovery, and search practices—and their implications for curriculum, conversation focused on related aspects of the field's communication practices, such as:

- Who owns information in the field? Who communicates it?
- How is information communicated in the field? How is it presented?
- Are special skills needed to present information? If yes, what are those skills? How is authority established?
- Do specialists in this field meet? Where? When? What do they do when they meet?
- How and by whom are valued information sources and collections in the field physically and digitally organized, stored, and accessed? (adapted from Lant 2001)

The outcomes of these wide ranging planning discussions, conducted over a several month period, ensured that research portal content would be seamlessly integrated into business course curricula, significantly enriched by library science. In addition, insights were incorporated from the Cal Poly study on students' varying conceptions about information and its use (Maybee 2006). Computer science students' recommendations on 'scaffolding' content provided further guidance for ensuring that student interactions with portal resources advanced discipline-specific inquiry, analysis, and communication capabilities (Somerville, Rogers, Mirijamdotter, & Partridge 2007).

Portal Design Processes

Through extensive dialogue, reflection, and action, collaboratively negotiated learning outcomes for both disciplinary mastery and information proficiencies were aligned with business departmental curriculum goals and university learning priorities. In addition, thoughtful reflection on aesthetic and navigation strategies guaranteed that the learning environment was well organized and intuitively comprehensible. Faculty involvement ensured that the portal content satisfied students' needs for general research guidance, including database listings, organized by core areas such as marketing, finance, management, and accounting. The portal also provided detailed research guidance—outlining essential research resources and techniques—for broad topical areas such as advertising, market share, and demographics. Furthermore, students received course-level research guidance through web pages customized to course assignments. Throughout, portal content and design aimed to advance course learning outcomes and department curricular objectives, as well as to meet accreditation agency standards.

Faculty members were highly engaged throughout the interactive design and development process. The first of several discrete consultation phases involved defining information and disciplinary competencies relevant to the business subject domain. Following this, task related skill sets were identified in terms of subject-specific information literacy competencies. Completion of this activity permitted creation of assignments that advanced core learning outcomes and employed appropriate teaching strategies. At this point, user-specific variables, such as prerequisite course content exposure, prior information instruction experiences, and specific task completion requirements, informed alignment of portal content, learning outcomes, instructional design, and assessment methods. In this way, Cal Poly computer science students' recommendations on content architecture informed decisions on learning style and class level design considerations. In addition, content presentation strategies deliberately acknowledged and advanced students' varying process, source, and purpose conceptions, thereby building on phenomenographic study insights.

Research Portal Integration

The teaching and learning value of the research portal is best illustrated through the experience of students enrolled in a course to obtain industry information during internships in the field. One student team was assigned a consultation with a local chocolate retailer who wanted to increase sales through a new marketing strategy. The client's long-term vision was to expand distribution from the local market to nation-wide distribution. Because all her chocolate ingredients were organic, she had a unique selling position.

This problem-based learning approach required that students substantively engaged in the often confusing and complex process of secondary marketing research. Success depended on application of core information literacy competencies and discipline-specific conceptions within an Internet mediated environment. In so doing, student learners were placed in a situation similar to what they would experience in the business world after graduation. However, in this case, the portal included a 'value added' course-specific research guide that provided research strategies and presented research tools relevant to the internship assignment.

The digital research portal design philosophy also intentionally reinforced field-based learning. By integrating business and information instruction within the context of use, the librarian maximized students' abilities to both recall and apply those concepts as they moved back and forth between academic and work worlds. Furthermore, through embedded integration of critical thinking skills into course learning outcomes, the research portal project simultaneously advanced both business and information competency.

This was demonstrated when students completed their preliminary environmental scans to identify priority issues for thorough investigation after consultation of the research portal. Following acquisition of needed information, students returned to the classroom where faculty facilitated data analysis and application with one or more environmental scanning tools.

Student learning assessment demonstrated that the combination of information and business competencies prepared students with skills transferable to conducting research on the variety of events, trends and relationships within organizations' internal and external environments. In enabling students to plan for future courses of action, the integration of the research portal into environmental scanning exercises thereby provided critical preparation for graduates' future success in the workplace.

Ongoing evaluation continues to inform portal improvements through an iterative design, creation, implementation, and management process, which ensures consistent alignment with evolving departmental learning goals. The requisite collaborative relationships provide contextualized guidance for cultivating the critical awareness of and experience with research tools necessary for graduates' success in information-intensive workplace environments.

The value of this approach is also underscored by new instances of faculty-initiated overtures to librarians, inviting them to co-design new curriculum approaches that better incorporate disciplinary research tools and advance transferable information literacy competencies. This phenomenon reflects faculty members' convictions that heightened abilities to identify and use information appreciably deepens students' learning, including markedly improved assignments.

Reflective Professional Action

Ever increasing user demand for value-added digital resources and enabling navigation assistance requires innovative thinking that harnesses the potential of web-based technologies. This accomplishment requires heightened collaboration between subject specialist librarians and disciplinary teaching faculty. In this research portal project, information literacy concepts were paired with core disciplinary content to accelerate students' interactions with digital research tools and business resource materials. Project outcomes reflect shared agreement that merely increasing the amount of information in the curriculum would not enhance student learning. In response, reflective conversations clarified the key understandings, ideas, themes, concepts, arguments, and solutions required for making explicit a fundamental and complementary cluster of abilities necessary to use disciplinary information effectively.

In this case, portal design and development assumed that information literacy is necessarily demonstrated in a situated context and within a content domain (Somerville & Vuotto 2005). The course content provided disciplinary fundamentals and the course assignments clarified professional practices. Within this information-based and learning-centered curricular framework, students advanced their information finding, evaluating, and using proficiencies. They developed sound investigatory methods, including critical discernment and reasoning. In addition, they deepened their appreciation for knowledge creation processes and information technology tools.

Through this process, information literacy was transformed from a library-owned concept into an essential graduate learning outcome. At the course level, this was expressed through detailed information-focused learning outcomes within course syllabi. At the department level, information competency was represented as a developmental sequence of learning that occurs throughout a program of study. Assessment activities increasingly involved librarians and professors in reviewing and assessing students' assignments together. This new instructional strategy advanced the library's contributions to the university's teaching and learning enterprise. And, through heightened collaboration, professors and librarians demonstrated the efficacy of advancing learning by inventing new ways of working together.

References

Australian and New Zealand Information Literacy Framework: Principles, Standards, and Practice. (2004). A. Bundy, ed., 2nd ed. Adelaide, Australia: Australian and New Zealand Institute for Information Literacy and Council of Australian University Librarians. Available: http://www.anziil.org/resources/Info%20lit%20 2nd%20edition.pdf

Bruce, C. (1997). The relational approach: A new model for information literacy. *The New Review of Information and Library Research, 3,* 3–22.

Catts, R. (2004). Preface. *Australian and New Zealand Information Literacy Frame-work: Principles, Standards, and Practice.* A. Bundy, ed., 2nd ed. Adelaide, Australia: Australian and New Zealand Institute for Information Literacy and Council of Australian University Librarians. Available: http://www.anziil.org/resources/Info%20lit%202nd%20edition.pdf

Lant, P. (2001). Information literacy and teaching with technology. University of Illinois Faculty Summer Institute on Learning Technologies. Unpublished paper.

Lupton, M. (2004). Overview. *Australian and New Zealand Information Literacy Framework: Principles, Standards, and Practice.* A. Bundy, ed., 2nd ed. Adelaide, Australia: Australian and New Zealand Institute for Information Literacy and Council of Australian University Librarians. Available: http://www.anziil.org/resources/Info%20lit%202nd%20edition.pdf

Maybee, C. (2006). Undergraduate perceptions of information use: The basis for creating user-centered student information literacy instruction. *Journal of Academic Librarianship*, 32(1), 79–85.

Partnership for 21st Century Skills. (2003). Learning for the 21st century: A report and mile guide for 21st century skills. Washington, D.C.: Partnership for 21st Century Skills.

Somerville, M. M., & Brar, N. (2009). A user-centered and evidence-based approach for digital library projects. *The Electronic Library*, 27(3), 409–425.

Somerville, M. M., Rogers, E., Mirijamdotter, A., & Partridge, H. (2007). Collaborative evidence-based information practice: The Cal Poly digital learning initiative. In E. Connor (Ed.), Evidence-Based Librarianship: *Case Studies and Active Learning Exercises* (pp. 141–161). Oxford, England: Chandos Publishing.

Somerville, M. M., & Vuotto, F. (2005). If you build it with them, they will come: Digital research portal design and development strategies. *Internet Reference Services Quarterly: A Journal of Innovative Information Practice, Technologies, and Resources*, 10(1), 77–94.

Vuotto, F. (2004). Information competence as a value-added product: Applying the business model to academe. *Reference Services Review* 32(3), 234–248.

Chapter Four
Learning Commons Synergies

The rapid emergence of peer production, social networking, and Internet technologies is reshaping the means by which information and culture are created and shared between individuals, groups, and societies. Reflective of these changes, members of the generation who have grown up with the Internet—referred to interchangeably as Millennials, the Net Generation, Generation Y, and the Digital Generation—create, distribute, share, and consume information (Lippincott 2007) in ways that challenge cherished higher education assumptions about learning, including libraries' traditional 'warehouse of knowledge' role.

In response, academic libraries increasingly serve as providers of space and resources that foster social interaction in physical and virtual learning environments (Somerville & Harlan 2008). Achieving the potential of these ambitious new opportunities requires reconsidering enshrined organizational planning models—including established notions about appropriate relationships between librarians, students, faculty, and other campus stakeholders (Somerville & Collins 2008). As the following account illustrates, librarians at California Polytechnic State University increasingly benefitted from user- and colleague-generated guidance through deepening collaborative relationships (Lippincott 2004).

Building It For Them

In 2003, the University President and Provost initiated the planning process for a campus learning commons to be constructed in repurposed space in the Library. The funding award stipulated that members of the faculty development center, university library, and campus technology services would collaboratively create the design concept. For over a year, members of these campus support units learned to work together. In the end, they agree on an integrated approach to improve teaching and revitalize curriculum. Their process was highly consultative, involving the campus' senior academic administrators, the academic senate technology committee, the council of college deans, and other campus governance and advisory bodies. All these entities approved the facility concept—to provide enabling technology infrastructure, pedagogical consultation, and scholarly resources (Gillette & Somerville 2006, Somerville & Gillette 2008). In addition, these faculty and administrative bodies approved the service concept—to encourage application of constructivist principles to advance students' information, communication, and technology proficiencies and thereby cultivate their transferable lifelong learning capabilities. The founding information, technology, and pedagogy partners thereby fulfilled the senior leaders' mandates.

After the learning commons opened, students were invited to conduct 'learn by doing' research investigations—so as to explicitly link the commons to learning (Lippincott 2006). Supervised by faculty, students generated research questions, selected research methodologies, and interpreted research data. Their research outcomes informed several recommendations which challenged the original faculty-focused approach envisioned by the learning commons planning team. For instance, students urged planners to expand the purpose of the commons. They recommended the creation of inclusive, interactive learning communities to facilitate cross-disciplinary communication (Somerville & Brar 2006). Illustrative of this concept, one student team proposed a senior project 'marketplace' to assist students in the completion of their capstone project. In assessing need and identifying user requirements, the research team determined that students would appreciably benefit from a comprehensive development and viewing tool for these senior projects. They arrived at these conclusions after employing a variety of research methods, including online surveys, focus groups, and participant observation.

Their data analysis confirmed that students wished to identify former senior projects in their area of interest, as well as former faculty supervisors for those projects. They also wished to identify other students currently interested in related subjects, since group work was permitted. In addition, students wished to have an online space where they could produce drafts of the senior project and receive faculty commentary. Upon completion, they wanted an easy means of submitting the final project and thereby satisfying this final graduation requirement. To design the desired system functionalities, the student team used a variety of design tools, including paper prototypes and usability studies.

This design concept presented a marked contrast to the existing senior project process. Projects, typically 'born digital,' were presented to library staff as paper print outs to be converted into microfiche. Only the briefest cataloging records were created—typically allowing only author and title access. Accessing earlier senior projects therefore required physically coming into the library building to locate appropriate fiche based on key words in the title. In some instances, retrieval was made more precise by a faculty referral to a specific student's senior project. A cumbersome microform reader was then required for viewing and, if desired, printing. Students unanimously stated that this laborious process discouraged benefitting from earlier students' work.

In presenting their ideas to learning commons planners, students also emphasized that peer production practices for social information exchange and knowledge production activities required that learning commons service providers must also include writing center experts, study skills specialists, and software training consultants. This advice served to enlarge the 'service circle' originally envisioned by the learning commons facility and service planners.

In addition, students recommended enhancements to the learning commons facility. For example, students in software engineering and artificial intelligence courses used 3-dimensional (3D) modeling techniques to design a variety of learning spaces—virtual collaboration rooms, a multimedia café, and a campus knowledge repository. They also implemented usability studies, focus groups, and online surveys to generate faculty- and student-generated ideas that both stimulated planners' reconsideration of design concepts and heightened their conversance with interactive design and evaluation techniques.

A significant difference in planner perspectives and student viewpoints involved the matter of formal and informal learning spaces. While learning commons planners had focused primarily on advancing students' formal learning activities, students recommended blending formal and informal learning experiences. The multimedia café proposal, for instance, included ready access to food and drink as well as relaxation and gaming opportunities. Students also advanced 'best practice' recommendations derived from industry standards set by Starbucks coffee houses and Barnes and Noble bookstores—further challenging the original design concept.

Among the several changes subsequently made, planners established a 'zone of innovation' to explore the efficacy of combining formal and informal learning activities. In the initial project, the Lumiere Ghosting Project used virtual reality production technologies to engage students working side-by-side with supervising faculty, university librarians, instructional designers, and technology experts. Team taught by professors of new media, architecture, and computer science, the course instructional design employed constructivist learning principles which intentionally built upon and extended students' prior understanding. The faculty also planned to facilitate frequent reflection and dialogue among student team members for the purpose of cultivating higher-order thinking and deeper learning in both formal (curricular) and informal (co-curricular) settings.

Lumiere Ghosting Project

The interactive media and information design course was a particularly suitable occupant for the 'zone of innovation' because the emerging field lacked an established curricular standard. Therefore, faculty members were free to invent curricular and co-curricular means of advancing student learning. Within that intellectual 'zone of innovation,' they decided to explore the application of narrative, including its theatrical forms, in the design of content for complex, interactive instructional systems. The course scope explicitly acknowledged the modern electronic culture which occupied much of students' out-of-class use of 'real world' technology tools. In addition, faculty expected students to integrate these technologies in a casual but innovative fashion into their coursework.

In advancing the learning commons' goal of encouraging pedagogical experimentation, the faculty teaching team envisioned a course design that embodied a wide range of theoretical approaches, cultural histories, and technology tools. They also intended for the course content to draw students directly into the central concerns of new media theory and development as well as learning theory and knowledge creation processes. Within this framework, faculty with expertise in technical writing, media theory, architectural design, and project development coached students over two semesters to create a new form of interactive theatre revolving around ghosts.

The Lumiere Ghosting Project recognized that since the invention of the motion picture camera by the Lumiere brothers, the world has been inundated with the 'ghosts' of moving cinematic images—Lumiere Ghosts. These iconic representations drift from culture to culture, from generation to generation. Sometimes they inhabit a physical form—a 'drag' performance of Marilyn Monroe in a Tokyo nightclub, for example—thereby altered, updated, and eventually set free again—perhaps through a video recording of the performance—to continue drifting across the electronic ether (movies, television, the Web) of modern culture. In preparing students to appreciate, analyze, and extend this phenomenon, faculty build a course syllabus that introduced students to media history, with a focus on the development of cinema, and with a survey of its accompanying theoretical structures for narrative and aesthetic analysis. At the same time, students were asked to design and build a physical space—a 'black box' media theatre—in which to demonstrate media transmission and media interpretation processes. In other words, students were asked to give a physical form to the ephemeral concept of the Lumiere Ghost. During the course of the project, students created, in essence, a sophisticated but deceptively simple haunted house.

The haunted house was named the Lumiere Ghosting Device and represented a new form of fully-immersive, interactive cinema. The interactive 3-dimensional cinema theatre in the Library learning commons connected to other Lumiere Ghosting Devices (theatres) through a high-speed connection to the Internet. In the final stage of the Project, students used the Library's Lumiere Ghosting Device to interact with other participants from distant locations. Live participants were represented as full-scale 3D interactive puppets (avatars) constructed from their actual images. All participants shared the use of a virtual environment common to each device, which could be repurposed for open collaboration, artistic expression, gaming, training, and interactive storytelling.

The Lumiere Ghosting Device essentially created a cinema-like environment in which participants could easily interact with participants from all over the globe. This system represented an innovative integration of live 3D digital imaging and display with non-invasive motion tracking technology, connected through a high speed Internet connection that allowed for seamless exchange of audio, video, and tracking data from one device to the next. Making use of recent developments in higher processing speeds, larger bandwidth capacities, and smaller computing and projection systems, the Lumiere Ghosting Device was designed to be portable so the entire device could be assembled, calibrated, and connected to the Internet by a small technical crew of three or four people working together in an afternoon.

Building It With Them

The Lumiere Ghosting Project is based on the pedagogical assumption that practice informs and builds upon a firm understanding of media theory and communication practice. In cultivating students' abilities as developers—in the role of script writer, production director, camera operator, video editor, and so on—faculty members intentionally moved them beyond uncritical consumption of the artifacts of this important form of cultural expression. As one professor stated of the current situation, "This is analogous to creating a populace that can read, but not write, and therefore can read the books in the library but have no hope of ever seeing a personal work set upon the shelves." In response, the Lumiere Ghosting Project placed the tools of production directly into students' hands. Furthermore, it strengthened students' knowledge of how digital systems can be used (and misused) for effective persuasion and for various forms of artistic, cultural, commercial, and political expression.

Toward that end, students learned about the process of new media design from the point of view of the artist, the storyteller, and the narrator, as well as from the perspectives of the audience member and the non-technologist. By combining technological invention with reflective analysis of theory and history, students became effective participants in the process of modern electronically-mediated discourse. Along the way, they developed capabilities transferable to other learning contexts, in and out of the 'formal' education system.

To prepare them for a world in which novices can become knowledge creators without completing arduous internships, faculty stimulated students' intellectual growth through opportunities to work first hand with new media technology. In an attempt to create newer, more powerful applications, they immersed students deeply into the problem solving process, forcing them to develop new conceptions of the world around them and question long-held assumptions about communication. These experiences allowed them to deepen their cognitive understanding of the moving image as a vital part of modern cultural expression.

Through extensive cross-disciplinary collaboration with students and faculty from widely divergent interests and backgrounds working together to create a single 'product', students and faculty evolved much more complex awareness of others' perspectives on the world as well as that of their academic fields. Working as part of a collaborative team encouraged students to develop a sense of social identity as professionals, artists and thinkers, and allowed them to develop a solid sense of belonging to a community that exists well outside the walls (actual and theoretical) of the university environment.

In addition, the necessity of meeting deadlines and producing collaborative products (software, hardware, architectural renderings) which must actually work and perform for an audience forced students to enhance self-awareness and self-efficacy while encouraging commitment to the group and to larger project goals, in combination with providing new avenues for self-expression. Because much of the teamwork for the technology development, testing and display process took place outside the standard "classroom" environment and was mostly negotiated through e-mail and other non-linear and asynchronistic forms of written and visual communication (including video conferencing and instant messaging), students strengthened the written, oral and visual presentation skills necessary to completing group tasks in contemporary work environments.

Consequently, at the conclusion of the one-year Lumiere Ghosting Project, students who had completed the entire curriculum obtained a thorough knowledge of how the moving image is integrated deeply into modern communication and learning processes and how the moving image presents itself across a wide range of mediums for a wide range of communicative and persuasive purposes. Students not only understood this in a general sense, but they could also evaluate the process as active participants in the process of 'making knowledge' with new media. As corroborated by faculty assessment of students' academic work, the rich blending of formal and informal learning afforded by the commons environment permitted students to appreciably further:

- **Research Competence**, as expressed through formulation of effective research questions and search strategies to inform Ghosting Device design and to develop Ghosting Project content,
- **Publishing Competence**, as revealed by explanations of how information is produced and exchanged to create knowledge within the media and communication field, including professional publications as well as Device R&D documentation,
- **Communication Competence**, as evidenced through selection of appropriate communication messages and dissemination channels to promote awareness of the Lumiere Ghosting Device demonstration project,
- **Social-structure Competence**, as demonstrated through contribution of original ideas into a community of inquiry, including Web-based systems, and

- **Technology Competence**, as demonstrated through effectively finding, organizing, and presenting data, information, and knowledge in the technology-enabled Lumiere Ghosting Device environment.

The location of the Lumiere Ghosting Project in the learning commons both provided the space and ensured the expertise necessary for accelerated student learning experiences. In addition, the project fostered a 'boundary crossing' community-of-practice among learning partners and faculty colleagues. Prompted by shared engagement in formal media development activities, collaborative learning arose from innovative integration of concrete experience, reflective observation, abstract conceptualization, and active experimentation (Gillette & Somerville 2006). Informal learning was also precipitated by casual conversations about the role of information and technology in contemporary knowledge production, dissemination, and management.

Building It For and With Them

The founding vision for the Cal Poly learning commons was set by senior academic administrators who intended to rejuvenate curriculum building practices. Toward that end, university leaders wished to promote faculty adoption of sound pedagogy, current research, and innovative technology. In this way, they planned to prepare graduates with the necessary skills and knowledge for successful lifelong learning in the digital age.

The 'zone of innovation' fulfilled the promise of this vision. New ways of working with students emerged as faculty collaboratively engaged in the construction of facts, ideas, concepts, theories, and experiences. Through formal and informal learning situations, faculty members interacted and shared with each other as they questioned, analyzed, debated, and negotiated learning and teaching ideas, including varying conceptions of information literacy (e.g., Bruce, Edwards, & Lupton 2006; Bruce 2008). Deep appreciation for the qualitatively different ways in which phenomena are conceived and experienced among different disciplines led to transformative changes in individual faculty members' approaches to teaching and learning.

The immersive commons learning environment moved participants beyond the mere intellectual aspects of engaging with information and creating knowledge to encompass the personal, practical, and social dimensions of engaging in a full 'learning life'. Through their own peer-to-peer experiences, faculty renewed their learning assumptions and revitalized their teaching approaches. In leveraging the power of collaborative learning to promote critical thinking and content expertise through faculty engagement in real world problems, this initiative demonstrated that students are not the only 'users' of a learning commons.

Library Learning Outcomes

The library offers an obvious venue where academic work can be conducted in a social context supported physically, intellectually, and remotely. The Lumiere Ghosting Project illustrates that library instruction programs need not be dominated by information resources and their delivery. Rather, redesigned educational models can incorporate a deeper understanding of the independent, active learning behavior of students and the evolving, responsive teaching strategies of faculty. Such redesigned approaches will recognize that the Net Generation values engagement for what it enables—customization, convenience, interaction, collaboration, experiencing, connectedness, and learning. This is oftentimes expressed through interactive team work. From this perspective, learning is a remarkable social process which, in truth, occurs not as a response to teaching but rather as a result of a social framework that fosters learning. As demonstrated in the Lumiere Ghosting Project, appreciation for and achievement of such potential learning is significantly furthered by robust collaboration partnerships and information practices.

References

Bruce, C. S. (2008). *Informed learning*. Chicago: Association of College and Research Libraries.

Bruce, C., Edwards, S., & Lupton, M. (2006). Six frames for information literacy education: A conceptual framework for interpreting the relationships between theory and practice. *Innovation in Teaching and Learning in Information and Computer Sciences*, 5(1, January), 1–18. Available: http://www.ics.heacademy.ac.uk/italics/vol5iss1.htm

Gillette, D. D., & Somerville, M. M.. (2006). Toward lifelong 'knowledge making': Faculty development for student learning in the Cal Poly learning commons. In D. Orr (Ed.), *Lifelong Learning: Partners, Pathways, and Pedagogies: Keynote and Refereed Papers from the 4th International Lifelong Learning Conference*, Yeppoon, Australia, (pp. 117–123). Rockhampton, Queensland, Australia: Central Queensland University.

Lippincott, J. K. (2006). Linking the information commons to learning. *Learning Spaces*, Diana G. Oblinger (Ed.) Boulder, Colorado: EDUCAUSE. Available: http://www.educause.edu/learningspaces.

Lippincott, J. K. (2004). New library facilities: Opportunities for collaboration. *Resource Sharing & Information Networks*, 17(1/2), 147–57.

Lippincott, J.K. (2007). Student content creators: Convergence of literacies. *EDUCAUSE Review*, Nov/Dec. Available: www.educause.edu/apps/er/erm07/erm07610.asp.

Somerville, M. M., & Brar, N. (2006). Collaborative co-design: The Cal Poly Digital

Teaching Library user centric approach. In *Information Access for Global Access: Proceedings of the International Conference on Digital Libraries (ICDL 2006)*, (pp. 175–187). New Delhi, India.

Somerville, M. M., & Collins, L. (2008). Collaborative design: A learner-centered library planning approach. *The Electronic Library, 26*(6), 803–820.

Somerville, M. M., & Gillette, D. D. (2008). The California Polytechnic State University Learning Commons: A case study. In B. Tierney & R. Bailey (Eds.), *Transforming Library Service Through Information Commons: Case Studies for the Digital Age* (pp. 43–47). Chicago: American Library Association.

Somerville, M. M., & Harlan, S. (2008). From information commons to learning commons and learning spaces: An evolutionary context, In (B. Schader (Ed.), *Learning Commons: Evolution and Collaborative Essentials* (pp. 1–36). Oxford, England: Chandos Publishing Ltd.

Chapter Five
Collaborative Workplace Systems

Through increasingly collaborative activities with faculty and students, librarians realized that it is the circulation of knowledge—not book circulation counts!—that produce learning (Bennett 2005). This insight challenged the adequacy of the library's traditional role as a repository of human culture. It required that the California Polytechnic State University Library evolve from a static resource center into a dynamic center of instruction, exploration, and learning.

In choosing to articulate, create, and sustain this bold aspiration, staff members built on other learning organization initiatives (e.g., Phipps 1993, 2001, 2004; Baughman & Hubbard 2001; Giesecke & McNeil 2004). As librarians considered how to proceed, they recalled enrichment gained through exposure to—and, increasingly, interaction with—stakeholders' perspectives during the digital learning environment (chapter 2), disciplinary research portal (chapter 3), and 'zone of innovation' (chapter 4) projects. Throughout, their engagement had been information-centered, learning-focused, and action-oriented. Projects had progressively expanded librarians' relationships with campus constituencies—moving them from receptive consumers to active co-creators.

In their initial work with computer science students, librarians benefitted from students' periodic written reports and oral presentations, culminating in end-of-the-quarter (re)design recommendations. Data was derived from a variety of sources—including focus groups, personal interviews, online surveys, and usability studies. Student researchers even convened librarians as a user group for an online catalog interface study. In an iterative fashion, paper prototypes were built and tested, using user-centric interaction design methods (Sharp, Rogers, & Preece 2007). Other projects conducted over a three year period yielded recommendations on the library website homepage (Gillette & Somerville 2005), bibliographic data visualization (Rogers 2005), information literacy program (Maybee 2006), and library space utilization (Somerville & Brar 2007). In all these instances, the librarians received secondary information only. They interpreted it as best they could, given that they had only 'second hand knowledge' of the research processes of identifying problems, formulating questions, determining methodology, selecting sources, collecting data, interpreting it, and so on.

In the case of the digital research portal, the business librarian assumed a collegial relationship with marketing faculty. He fully participated in question setting, information identification, and source evaluation. The project outcome—a disciplinary research portal (Somerville & Vuotto 2005)—reflected months of negotiation, including 'value added' consideration of the field's knowledge structure in the context of its creation processes (Lant 2001). The extensive dialogue enriched the librarian's conversation with marketing literature and curriculum objectives. In turn, the librarian extended faculty colleagues' understanding of scholarly communication patterns and practices, including a bibliographic system for organizing knowledge and accessing information. Because faculty were convinced that learning facilitates seeing the world in new ways (Marton & Booth 1997), they agreed that students should explicitly develop more complex ways of working with information, so as to become informed learners. From a discipline perspective, this could relate to students' understanding of particular topic areas or to the wider discipline. From the information use perspective, this may relate to their experience of the profession's information practices, their practice applying disciplinary research methodologies, or their renegotiation of academic information boundaries (Bruce 2008). Portal content, therefore, was designed to advance students' conversation with both knowledge structure and disciplinary content. In doing so, it mirrored the redesigned curriculum.

Since organizational and individual change begins with the outset of research, these incrementally participatory research experiences prompted librarians' recognition that the question of what to study was critically important. As their experiences revealed, it is equally important to consider the question of how—and with whom—to conduct research studies. Initially, the university's 'learn by doing' educational philosophy informed librarians' invitation of student-generated research projects to obtain authentic perspectives on 'user experiences'. This approach requires relinquishing control of the research process: students, with faculty supervision, generated problem definitions, chose research methodologies, conducted data analysis, and produced results reports. Following this, librarians conversed with student researchers and faculty supervisors to 'make sense' of research findings in terms that informed system modifications and organizational changes. Through these early experiences, the iterative dialogue inherent in collaborative design processes fostered sustainable communications which altered relationships, processes, and practices for librarians and their campus beneficiaries. Professional frameworks shifted from 'library centric' to 'user centric' and 'habits of mind' increasingly embraced inclusive practices and diverse viewpoints. Over time, librarians negotiated faculty partnerships that permitted them to significantly influence curriculum content and delivery.

The campus benefits of these collaboration relationships were certainly considerable. However, few librarians were substantively involved in the research study implementations. Therefore, among those with only 'second hand' experiences, considerable collective yearning developed for substantial engagement in original inquiry. Mindful of the social nature of learning—i.e., that all learning derives from experience, one's own and others (Ackoff 1999), librarians expressed an unsatisfied desire for inclusive research methods capable of furthering both collective understanding and situation improvement. In addition, since librarians lacked a means of guaranteeing either inquiry or relationships with campus collaborators after project conclusion, they also sought to create workplace learning structures and collaborative practices supportive of enabling perpetual inquiry and continuous communication.

Participatory Action Research

With these methodological characteristics in mind, participants chose to employ participatory action research for their learning journey. There are various forms and definitions for action research (e.g., Checkland & Holwell 1998a, Dick 2004, Rapoport 1970) but, generally speaking, the action researcher's role is to create organizational change while simultaneously studying the process. Therefore, the action researcher becomes part of the study and interprets the inter-subjective meaning of the observations. Despite the variety in action research approaches, they have in common a cyclic process where the 'systemic' research cycle consists of situation diagnosis, action planning, and action taking (intervening), followed by evaluating and reflecting—i.e., learning (Susman & Evered 1978).

Participatory action research is a form of action research that involves practitioners as both subjects and co-researchers (Argyris & Schön 1991) in "collaborative processes aimed at improving and understanding their worlds in order to change them" (McIntrye 2008, ix). This departs from other types of applied research where the researcher is seen as the expert (Whyte, Greenwood, & Lazes 1991). In contrast, participatory action research aims to construct an environment where participants freely exchange information and make informed choices, thereby promoting commitment to the investigation results (Argyris & Schön 1991.) Through co-constructing, testing and improving theories about particular interpretations and experiences, people learn by interacting with each other that they can better control their social world (Elden & Levin 1991).

An additional characteristic of action research addresses issues of validity and reliability: the action research process must be sufficiently transparent to make it, in principle, recoverable (Checkland & Holwell 1998b). This requires explicitly describing elements that, in fact, are relevant to any piece of research, as reflected in Figure 1.

The figure illustrates how any research may be thought of as entailing three main elements. Theories or particular linked ideas (Framework of ideas—F) are used in a Methodology (M) to investigate an Area of concern (A). Using a methodology, such as one that builds on action research, may then yield lessons not only about A but also about the M and its adequacy in relation to F and A. So it is essential to declare in advance the elements of F, M, and A in Figure 1

Figure 1. The F-M-A Framework (after Checkland & Holwell 1998b, 13)

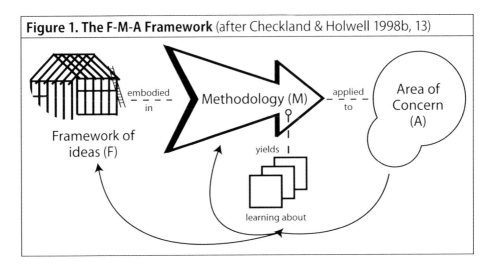

because, without such a declaration, the outcome cannot be considered research findings and research lessons. This definition constitutes the epistemology for recognizing knowledge created through action research.

In this case, the Area of concern is the changes in how information is produced, as well as how it is organized and accessed, which in turn challenges libraries' traditional roles, forcing librarians and staff to evolve in response to changing situations. The guiding Framework of ideas for enabling this organizational initiative is participatory action research combined with systems thinking, specifically, Soft Systems Methodology.

Systems Thinking Fundamentals

Cal Poly practitioners recognized the benefits of the action-oriented projects which had produced improved search interfaces, research portals, and learning environments. At the same time, they recognized that they had no means of consistently extending relationships—and, hence, collectively communicating and learning—beyond the conclusion of the project. Nor did they have a ready means of integrating insights from these various projects into a 'holistic' understanding of the organization's internal and external circumstances. As a result, they lacked a 'big picture' framework to inform organizational design decisions, human resource allocations, political negotiation strategies, and workplace culture attributes (Bolman & Deal 2008). This situation prompted their readiness to combine systems thinking and action research, as recommended by a number of experts (Checkland 1985, Flood 1998, Midgley 2000, Wilson 2001).

As the name suggests, systems thinking encourages viewing the organization as an enterprise level organism. Systems thinking methodologies enable appreciation of the interdependent relationships with customers, suppliers, and other stakeholders and encourage focus on the purpose, or function, of the part within the whole—including analysis of influential internal and external environmental factors (e.g., Checkland 1981, Churchman 1971, Churchman 1984). It recognizes that holistic systems thinking must be ongoing in organizations if participants are to function, aligned, as effective parts of the whole (Davis & Somerville 2006). Additionally, as this approach requires renegotiation of the boundaries of influence and concern, it also assures reflection on organizational culture, systems, and structures. Therefore, systems thinking served both as a fundamental underpinning of this organizational change initiative and also informed selection of a participatory action research approach.

While a variety of systems thinking-based methodologies exist (Jackson 2003), Soft Systems Methodology (SSM) was selected because, by its very nature, it creates a relational context that encourages participants to recognize their workplace expertise which, if shared, advances group understanding (Checkland & Scholes 1990, Checkland 1999, Checkland 2000). The methodology has been in development for over thirty years by Dr. Peter Checkland at the University of Lancaster in the United Kingdom. Mainly used in the areas of management and information systems development, its underlying constructivist philosophy reinforces the notion that people who want to improve a situation perceived as problematic can make improvements, or changes, through 'learning their way'

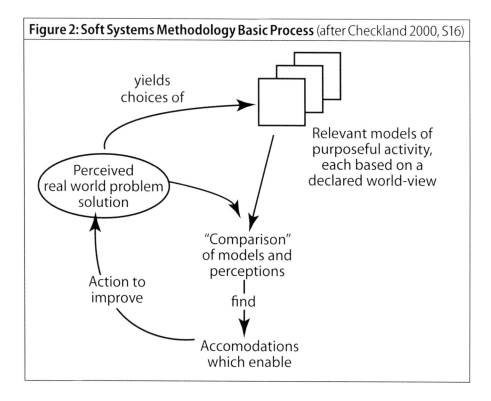

Figure 2: Soft Systems Methodology Basic Process (after Checkland 2000, S16)

yields choices of

Relevant models of purposeful activity, each based on a declared world-view

Perceived real world problem solution

"Comparison" of models and perceptions

Action to improve

find

Accomodations which enable

to 'taking actions to improve' (Checkland & Poulter 2006). Using a variety of tools, SSM thinking processes guide dialogue-based (Jenlink & Banathy 2005) appreciative inquiry (Checkland & Cesar 1986; Vickers 1983a, 1983b) which furthers organizational learning.

This systems thinking approach is commonly described as comprising an iterative four-stage process—finding out, modeling, comparison, and taking action—as depicted in Figure 2. Within each stage, some techniques are commonly used to support the process. For instance, Rich Pictures are often used to structure the data and impressions at the finding out stage of exploring perceptions in the 'real-world problem situation'. The main idea in using Rich Picture building is to present structures and processes relevant to the situation under study and depict these, including relationships, within the 'climate' in which they exist.

In modeling purposeful activity, the second stage, some precise techniques—Root Definition and Activity Models—are used to further build systems thinking proficiencies. The Root Definition states what the system 'is.' It is based on elements that specify customer, actor, owner, worldview, process and constraints for the situation or system under study. The Activity Model shows how the system carries out the process stated in the Root Definition and how such a process would be judged in principle. The outcome of the modeling stage is then compared against perceptions of the real-world situation to find issues and suggestions for improvements. In the comparison stage, participants seek an accommodation of desirable and feasible changes which are then implemented, and a new cycle begins.

This learning cycle consists of problem formulation, information gathering, interpretative analysis, and action taking. Although the cycle is explained above in linear terms, in practice there is significant iteration within the cycle as group learning occurs. Also, taking action to improve the problematical situation will, of course, change the situation, so that the learning cycle could in principle again. "In this sense, SSM's learning cycle can be seen a never-ending. It ultimately offers a way of continuously managing any ongoing human situation. It does this by helping understanding of complex situations, encouraging multiple perspectives to be taken into account, and bringing rigor to processes of analysis, debate and taking 'action to improve' (Checkland & Poulter 2006, p. xvii-xviii), as depicted in Figure 3.

This cycle is typically introduced into organizations by external consultants. It guides participant learning for the duration of the project. Then, when the consultants leave, explicit critical thinking activities cease. In departing from this usual pattern, Cal Poly participants committed to continue exercising explicit 'better thinking' processes (Somerville & Mirijamdotter 2005).

Staff members also recognized the importance of both activating and coordinating individual learning to advance organizational learning (Stacey 2003,

Figure 3. SSM's Cycle of Learning for Action (from Checkland & Poulter 2006, xix)

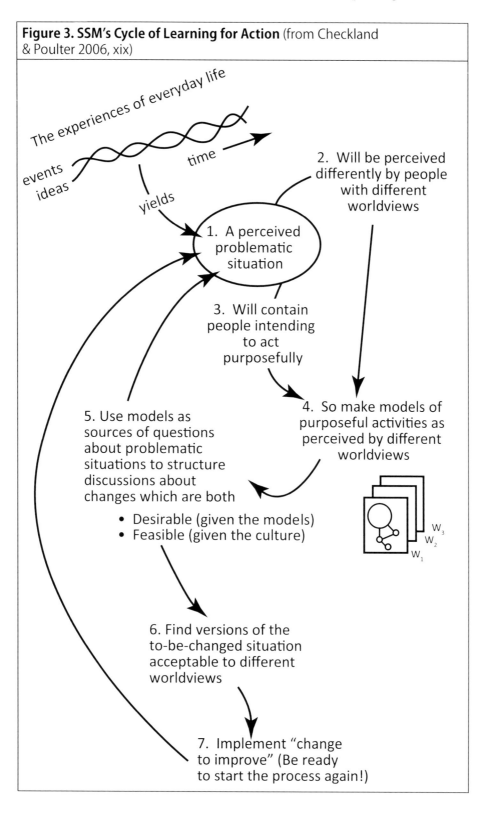

2004) through interactive communication (Varey 2005) guided by shared vision, values, and goals (Davis & Somerville 2006). By encouraging the intentional sharing of information, knowledge, skills, and abilities, in the form of questioning, evaluating and reflecting, they aspired to enable nimble organizational improvement amidst dynamic environmental change. This inquiry-based approach had the added benefit of involving participants in consideration of the social dimension of learning, the diversity of learner needs, and the fostering of self-sufficiency and lifelong learning—factors of critical importance in determining libraries' future roles.

RISE Information System

In keeping with the learn-by-doing educational philosophy of the polytechnic university, action research outcomes simultaneously brought about change in the project situation (the action) while participants learned from the process of deriving the change (the research) (Wilson, 2001). The iterative nature of the action research cycle both ensured rich workplace learning experiences and also informed incremental problem situation improvements. In the initial learning project, for instance, staff collaboratively designed and developed an interactive information storage and retrieval system.

This project had its origins in a study of reference desk transactions conducted during fall quarter 2003. Results revealed that eighteen percent of inquires were directional queries, twenty-two percent concerned equipment problems, fifty-six percent were informational questions, and four percent were otherwise classified. Of the informational queries, fifty-one percent were assignment related and thirty-three percent involved either known item searches or ready reference business questions. Through SSM-guided dialogue, reference librarians reflected upon the implications of these findings in the light of campus knowledge management and digital migration priorities. Concurrently, elsewhere in the library organization, usage data at two redundant public information desks prompted their closure, encouraging recognition that 'back room' technical services staff and 'displaced' public services staff could successfully field 'first contact' reference inquiries if they were prepared to do so.

Launched in January 2004, the reference desk pilot project was named Research Information Services and Education (RISE) by the paraprofessionals reassigned there. To prepare staff for their new assignment, the former reference librarians agreed to provide course assignments and coaching strategies for assisting students at the reference desk. In response to transaction findings, librarians also delivered in depth instruction on the intricacies of searching high demand databases, supplemented by intensive business research education. Ongoing reference desk question analysis prompted presentations, as well, from other library units including interlibrary loan, digital services, e-reserve, and special collections. Over time, a library wide communication network evolved, focused on student learning and enabled by formal and informal information exchange.

With an increasing understanding of the academic enterprise, RISE staff also used research evidence over a several month period to produce the socio-technical specifications for a decision-support database and information exchange forum (Somerville & Vazquez 2004; Somerville, Huston, & Mirijamdotter 2005). In an early effort to articulate functional system requirements in the light of RISE purposes, relationships, and processes, paraprofessional staff—referred to here as 'library assistants'—drew Figure 4 at the start of the project. The simple drawing acknowledges the fledgling exchange relationships between librarians and library assistants and their shared interest in the reference desk support system. The rendering also conveys the beginning of a two-way relationship between participants in the socio-technical RISE system and the learning, teaching, and research activities that drive the academic enterprise.

After eight months of systems thinking practice, RISE staff produced a drawing which reveals 'deep learning' about enterprise-level library purposes, processes, and interrelationships. It also reflects an improved ability to conduct

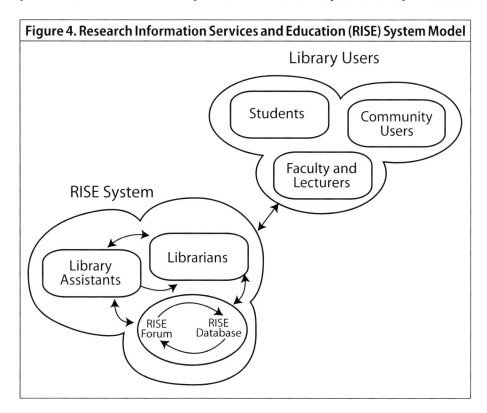

Figure 4. Research Information Services and Education (RISE) System Model

data analysis and evaluate service success. As depicted in Figure 5, participants understand the socio-technical RISE decision support system to be a communication and collaboration tool. The database system is understood in terms of higher-level system functions. 'Capture customers inquiries' refers to assignments obtained by librarians from faculty and forwarded to the database in advance of their distribution to students. 'Capture situated knowledge' acknowledges librarians' formal and informal contextualization of assignment purposes. 'Capture information search process' refers to librarians' written recommendations for 'first contact' assistance, supplemented if needed by formal instruction during weekly staff meetings. Staff members also recognize the value of purposeful dialogue among staff and between staff and librarians, as

Figure 5. Research Information Services and Education (RISE) Human Activity Model

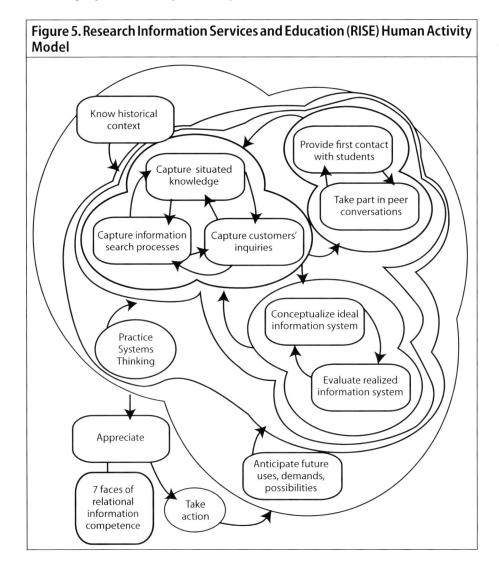

indicated by the phrase 'take part in peer conversations'—including the RISE system 'forum'.

For the final element of the socio-technical system, staff chose the relational information literacy concepts (Bruce 1997a, 1997b) advanced in the second edition of the *Australian and New Zealand Information Literacy Framework: Principles, Standards, and Practices* (Bundy 2004) to evaluate efficacy and propose enhancements. ANZIIL standards also guided assessment of RISE staff learning by an outside evaluator who recognized that relational "information literacy is necessarily demonstrated in a context and within a domain of content" (Catts 2004, p. 2). In addition, the framework was used to explicitly generate learning outcomes for RISE staff training and education which enabled them to advance users' information literacy capabilities.

The ANZIIL *Framework* also informed the next phase of the pilot project when technical services paraprofessionals joined the RISE team. Having each accrued between fifteen and thirty-two years of technical services' experience, these staff members possessed significant cataloging and processing expertise. Here-to-fore, however, these proficiencies had only been applied to building the 'back end' of the library's online public access catalog (OPAC) and ensuring shelf-ready monographic and serials holdings—i.e., their duties were limited to activities that precluded contact with the public.

To activate and extend their prior learning, a course was planned for delivery by librarians in four-hour sessions over a six-week period during July and August 2004. The curriculum was constructed from an analysis of what staff would need to know to successfully advise students. Learning outcomes and course materials were obtained from the assignments captured in the RISE system database, supplemented by information gleaned from extensive study of reference questions. These queries and assignments also provided the source material with which staff practiced their research and consultation reference interview skills (Somerville, Schader, & Huston 2005).

At the start of the 24-hour course, participants analyzed the structural components of students' capstone senior projects for the purpose of appreciating what undergraduate users need to know at graduation. Staff discovered that this culminating requirement assumes disciplinary mastery as well as information literacy, critical thinking, and writing abilities. Newly oriented, RISE staff members understood that the outcome of their work must demonstrably contribute to students' advancement of the knowledge, skills, and abilities necessary to successful completion of this graduation requirement. As the course participants' responsibilities included cataloguing and processing senior projects, this exercise stimulated a new user-centered perspective on a familiar bibliographic item which assumed new importance as a 'learning object' for them.

Building upon this emerging point of view, staff next identified all the points in the senior project process where students might come to the library reference desk to seek assistance. This activity continued to build insights into users' experiences. Rethinking through a familiar artefact re-examined in a new light advanced their appreciation for the role of information in learning, concurrent with extending staff perceptions of their transferable expertise.

Longitudinal self report and external evaluator findings revealed that, since joining the team in September 2004, the technical services RISE staff members have appreciably enhanced reference service quality. They regularly apply their in-depth knowledge of OPAC record-creation and their ever evolving capabilities in enhancing discovery and usage of licensed databases and search engines. The RISE database and forum have also benefited from the new bibliographic and technical expertise on the team; enhancements include improved database architecture, information visualization, and search functionalities. Even more importantly, the conversations leading to improvements in the RISE system 'learning object' have fostered conversations which established the trust and caring needed to encourage rethinking other library purposes, relationships, processes, and boundaries, using common language and shared tools.

Knowledge Management Initiative

In a second project begun when RISE staff assumed their duties at the reference desk, librarians initiated a yearlong process to prepare themselves for delivery of knowledge management services and products. This re-orientation required moving beyond traditional and relatively passive library centric professional boundaries to re-purpose, rethink, and retool. Change occurred through practice-inspired research about and with users, including Web-based research guides which served as the 'learning object'.

Soft Systems Methodology (SSM) thinking tools guided work, including intentional advancement of information competence and knowledge creation proficiencies. This focus mirrors the growing recognition—documented in a small but important literature—that information literacy capabilities are becoming increasingly critical to organizational success as well as professional practice. Research into the role of relational information literacy—which recognizes that proficiency best advances concurrent with domain knowledge—has occurred in a few fields (Bruce 1999; Kuhlthau 1999; Kuhlthau & Tama 2001; Smith & Martina 2004; Cheuk 1998a, 1998b, 2000, 2002; Lloyd 2004, 2005a, 2005b; Al-Daihari & Rehman 2007). In this instance, librarians sought to apply this learning framework to organize and enrich virtual information and knowledge space (Materska 2004). In the process, they reinvented their work purposes and processes.

To transition from a service to a learning orientation, project participants were guided in their rethinking by the holistic framework of Soft Systems Methodology. The librarians used SSM to provide common language and shared tools for discussion and analysis of project complexities and relational interdependencies. In addition, the constitutive elements of SSM—finding out, modeling, comparing, and taking action—guided seeking and evaluating meaningful data, comparing and contrasting multiple interpretations, and infusing reflective insights and curiosities into ongoing workplace learning processes.

For three months, librarians initiated discovery by making 'house calls' to academic departments, where they improved their understanding of the curriculum in terms that informed both collection development and information instruction activities. In conversation with faculty colleagues (Bechtel 1986), they studied college and department mission statements, curriculum plans, accreditation requirements, and course syllabi. Librarians then applied these insights to write content for discipline specific web research guides. These activities prompted discussion about professional assumptions, values, and priorities, in the light of the library's emerging new strategic directions. Their intention to significantly advance student learning also led to reflection on professional purposes and outcomes, roles and responsibilities, collegiality and collaboration, and communication and dialogue (Mirijamdotter & Somerville 2005).

As a result, librarians re-invented their roles and responsibilities, including this suite of outreach services:

- Review of course assignments and syllabi with academic faculty to explore possibilities for leveraging new information resources and finding aids to reconstruct assignments;
- Review of academic departments' mission and vision, curriculum plans, external reviews, and accreditation standards, complimented by ongoing conversations with academic department liaisons to ensure collection development profile currency;
- Pairing of disciplinary information resources and research competencies with curriculum integration strategies which successfully advance information, communication, and technology proficiencies among students and faculty; and
- Dialogue with college faculty members to embed information competence proficiencies and information resource content into revised course syllabi and departmental curricula.

Librarians also re-engaged with the research results generated earlier by students about students. In preparation, they used a Soft Systems Methodology systems thinking tool, the Rich Picture, to depict undergraduate students' information source experiences, as revealed early on in a study of undergraduate students' information conceptions (Maybee 2006). The group activity provided an opportunity to compare what students know upon entering college with what they need to know to graduate. This conversation—guided by the drawing depicted in Figure 6—naturally led to consideration of appropriate means of aiding students to acquire necessary familiarity with journals and other scholarly resources.

Recalling student researchers' strong recommendations that the library enhance its web presence, librarians next addressed adoption of student-generated web research guide templates (Rogers, Somerville, & Randles 2005). Since the web pages reside within the Cal Poly website, librarians also considered students' related recommendations on both university and library web site content and navigation (Gillette & Somerville 2005). This review served as the catalyst for a comprehensive redesign of the university library website, in which librarians assumed new roles as content providers and information architects for digital learning environments (Somerville, Mirijamdotter, & Collins 2006).

In assuming these new organizational roles, librarians demonstrated increased conversance with interaction design (Cooper & Reimann 2003) and usability testing (Barnum 2001) fundamentals as well as user experience (Krug 2005)

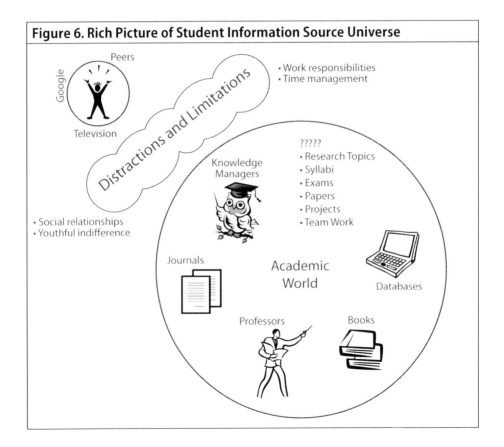

Figure 6. Rich Picture of Student Information Source Universe

and information encounter (e.g., Morville 2005) consequences. Their knowledge integration activities are best captured by a Soft Systems Methodology thinking tool, "Processes for Organizational Meaning" (POM), which reflects information and communication interactions underlying collaborative information exchange and knowledge creation (Mirijamdotter & Somerville 2005).

As depicted in Figure 7, this model identifies seven thinking elements derived from Checkland's Soft Systems Methodology (SSM) and furthered by Vickers' concept of an appreciative system (Checkland 1994; Checkland & Casar 1986). Both theories address the relationship-maintaining aspects of organizations and the underlying social, cultural, and political contexts. Elements 1-2 represent sources for identification of relevant environmental elements, so-called 'capta' (Checkland & Holwell 1998b), which both depends upon and extends project participants' data collection and analysis expertise. The notion is that information exchange drives ongoing processes of creating meaning through dialogue and reflection that nurtures understanding, as expressed in elements 3-4-5. This

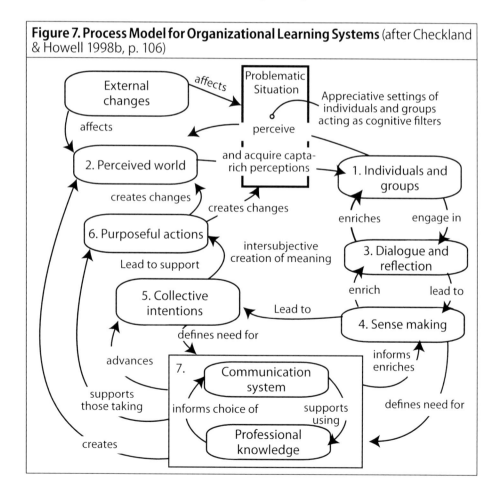

Figure 7. Process Model for Organizational Learning Systems (after Checkland & Howell 1998b, p. 106)

intends to affect collaborators' appreciative settings. It follows that dialogue and negotiation processes inform purposeful actions (element 6), based on accommodated views. Shared understanding also furthers—and is furthered by—organizational information systems that advance professional purposes (element 7), by means of which needed social and technical learning occurs, iteratively, through recurring processes.

While the SSM process model originated in the information systems field, it also proved to be transferable to guiding librarians' group learning within a library setting. Its holistic framework reminded participants of the importance of purposeful communication and dialogue to further collaborative creation of shared reality and common meaning. In valuing inclusive participation, the model honored the mental constructs that co-workers generated to understand—or to obtain an improved understanding—of a situation. Participants appreciated that these mental constructs are largely constructed by individual worldviews, perceptions, and values that, in turn, are based on individual background and previous experience. These ideas correspond to the concept of social-cultural learning, which is the essence of collaborative learning. As the figure anticipates, this iterative cycle of activating and enabling purposeful action and interactive evaluation will produce changes in understanding—i.e., learning—through a variety of information exchange and knowledge creation experiences.

These learning activities readied librarians to invent and deliver an academic knowledge management program. Their new responsibilities encompassed face-to-face and virtual information literacy education and research consultation, complimented by learning-focused collections development and collaborative learning environment design and development. These responsibilities replaced librarians' earlier preoccupation with 'sitting at the reference desk' and 'one-shot' bibliographic instruction sessions. As librarians grew more confident in expressing new professional purposes, work processes, and workplace relationships, they progressively improved alignment with the university's core teaching, learning, and research mission (Davis & Somerville 2006).

Organizational Learning Assessment

In an assessment session held at the conclusion of this three year action research study, an external evaluator invited participants to apply 'soft' systems principles and practices to depict their enlarged workplace context. Their conceptions were captured in visual drawings which provided a common reference for renegotiating increasingly more complex and better contextualized organizational effectiveness, as well as larger boundaries of influence and

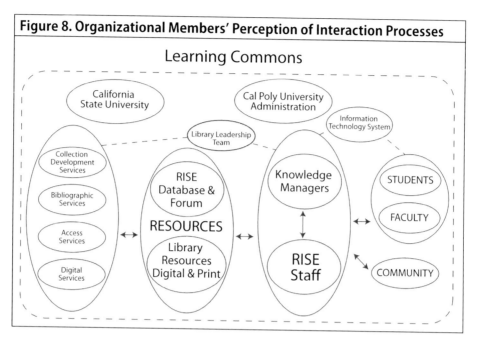

Figure 8. Organizational Members' Perception of Interaction Processes

concern. Illustrative of the renderings, the Rich Picture in Figure 8 presents an enterprise level model of university interactions—including consideration of what parts and relations to include—e.g., hierarchical levels, main processes, primary beneficiaries, relevant perspectives, and leading questions.

Figure 8 illustrates the new workplace environment enabled by rethinking activities. For instance, the librarians refer to themselves as Knowledge Managers. They reside in the same circle as RISE 2, an enlarged group of information and instructional services support staff. To the right, the importance of relationships with students and faculty are recognized. Another circle indicates the need to also serve the community. The drawing on the left indicates recognition that both these groups, librarians/knowledge managers and research information and instructional services/paraprofessional staff, interact with (increasingly digital) information resources which, the left most drawing illustrates, are acquired and organized by collection development and bibliographic services staff and made accessible by information technology (digital services) and access services specialists. Finally, at the top of the figure, the relationships with university administrators, campus information technologists, and library leaders are acknowledged, as is the California State University system in which Cal Poly serves as one of twenty three campuses. This high level 'system' is termed 'Learning Commons'—a phrase which refers to a physical, technological, social, and intellectual place (or space) for collaborative learning (Somerville & Harlan 2008). In the view of project participants, the Cal Poly library environment had become a physical and virtual learning commons over the course of the initiative.

Before this project began, workplace participants had never collectively reflected on their roles in a holistic context. As Figure 8 demonstrates, one of the most profound outcomes of this three year rethinking project is clarification of workplace participants' relationships to internal and external stakeholders. These insights emerge quite naturally, as one of the defining characteristics of SSM practice is intentionally entertaining multiple perspectives. Furthermore, by its very nature, Soft Systems Methodology creates a relational context that encourages individuals' recognition of the aspects of their workplace expertise which, when shared, advances collective knowledge creation and integration (Checkland 2000), even as it extends boundaries of influence and concern.

Organizational learning is also revealed through comparison of the Rich Pictures generated over the course of the project by library participants. These images demonstrate the maturation indicators that, early on, librarians agreed were significant to student learning. They were therefore able, at project's end, to appreciate their own learning in these terms: learning is about change in conceptions, learning always has content as well as process, learning is embodied in the relationship between the learner and the subject matter, and advancement of learning depends on the readiness to change perspectives.

As documented in external evaluator evaluations, information literacy and systems thinking frameworks, principles, and practices increasingly guided individual and group learning discussions. Collegial dialogue was enriched by explicit acknowledgement of enterprise-level mission and vision priorities. Individual and collective information experiences were discussed in terms of information seeking, evaluating, organizing, and reporting expectations. Collaborative information practices aspired to frame good questions, identify authoritative information, compare plausible interpretations, and weigh possible communication strategies. The application of these professional attributes in house anticipated increasing need among campus constituencies for these critical contributions to the knowledge creation, organization, and dissemination activities underpinning teaching, learning, and researching. Toward that end, as better thinking capabilities were integrated into daily work habits, individuals reported increasing confidence in demonstrating '21st Century learning and information literacy' (Breivik 2005)—i.e., recognizing pivotal questions and initiating inquiries, seeking and evaluating meaningful data, comparing and contrasting multiple interpretations, and infusing reflective insights and unsolved curiosities into a continuous learning process.

Organizational Leadership Implications

In order for these 21st Century attributes to be expressed and sustained, the design of workplace environments must support information encounters that enable employees to find the possibilities, energize the vision, and create the future. Within such a robust learning milieu, both the nature of organizational information and the purpose of organizational work can be revisited. As participants explore the complexity of the organization and its situation, they learn to diagnose problems, identify consequences, and make informed responses within a holistic context. This changes how people think and what they think about: individuals see the underlying context and assumptions for decisions. This new relational understanding predisposes individuals to adjust assumptions and strategies as their appreciative settings change.

With the conviction that "if organizations are constructed, they can be reconstructed" (Norum 2002, 424), Cal Poly library administrators recognized the importance of decentralizing the role of leadership to enhance the capacity of all employees to work productively toward common goals. To accomplish this, they recognized that they had to reframe the 'hows and whys' of leadership (Pearce & Conger 2003). Because organizations need to be flexible, adaptive, and productive in situations of rapid change, they understood that employees must "continually expand their capacity to create the results they truly desire, where new and expansive patterns of thinking are nurtured, where collective aspirations are set free, and where people are continually learning to see the whole together" (Senge 1990, 3). For this to occur, administrators have to "discover how to tap people's commitment and capacity to learn at all levels" (ibid. 4).

This required redesigning organizational structures which were not conducive to reflection and engagement. It also necessitated providing people with the thinking tools and guiding ideas to make sense of their situations, in the spirit of 'shared leadership' (Deiss & Sullivan 1998; Pan, Howard, Somerville, & Mirijamdotter 2009). In this instance, dialogue-based action research encouraged librarians to move beyond the constraints imposed by years (in some cases, more than three decades) of "sitting at the reference desk" and pointing at bibliographic finding tools—but not entering substantively into the teaching and learning processes (Somerville & Schader 2005). In sharp contrast, sustained dialogue with faculty subsequently produced information rich critical thinking assignments with explicit and measurable learning outcomes (e.g., Elrod & Somerville 2007) that accelerate discipline-based 'informed learning' (Bruce 2008). This came about when librarians initiated 'embedding' strategies (Dewey 2004) that engaged professors in working together with librarians to advance students' capabilities as information consumers and knowledge creators.

This change required transformation of thinking about organizational role and responsibilities, including renegotiation of the boundaries of influence and concern, purposes and outcomes, roles and responsibilities, collegiality and collaboration, and communication and exchange. The model, Figure 9, illustrates the responsibilities of the organizational leader who chooses to enable, employ, and implement action oriented systems thinking practices and processes. It represents layers of activities that interact with each other.

At the very center of the figure, activity 1 represents the activities that are involved in providing an active learning environment. Its placement at the very heart of the model conveys the belief that a contemporary organization should be designed to rapidly learn from and adapt to its own successes and failures, and those of relevant others. It should also be capable of adapting to internal and external changes that affect its performance, and of anticipating such changes and taking appropriate action before these changes occur. This requires, among other things, that the organization remain susceptible to continual redesign by its internal and external stakeholders (Ackoff, Magidson, & Addison 2006).

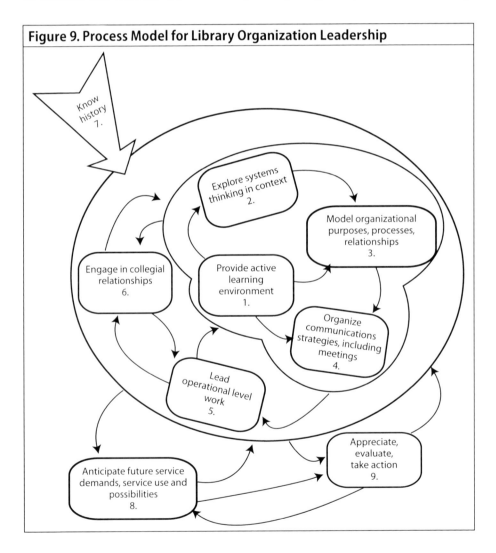

Figure 9. Process Model for Library Organization Leadership

Therefore, the organizational leader should create the conditions for employees to easily access and exchange information in terms that extend their interpretive and appreciative capabilities. Accomplishing this requires understanding "the process through which an organization (re)constructs knowledge" (Huysman & de Wit, 2003, 29)—i.e., organizational learning.

The figure recognizes that active learning environments allow practice in systems thinking, activity 2. The leader advances systems thinking within the organizational context to further the understanding of its parts and their inter-relations. Linked to systems thinking and also team success is the shared vision (Senge 1990) that informs activity 3, modeling of the organizational mission in both formal and informal settings including 'sense making' conversations. The final activity on this level, activity 4, illustrates that physical and virtual meetings are vital for facilitating active and dynamical engagement in information exchange. In this instance, interactive SSM processes enabled both redefinition of the organizational purposes and also redesign of the workplace environment, including the learning processes through which organizational purposes are reconsidered (Checkland & Winter 2006).

For the sake of model completeness, activity 5 recognizes the importance of leading operational level work. Its counterpart, activity 6, refers to engagement in internal and external relationship building. Historical context, activity 7, represents understanding how and why the present situation has come into being. This perspective offers relational context for envisioning the future, activity 8, including anticipated services and systems.

Finally, processes and outcomes need to be appreciated in the light of organizational purpose and vision, activity 9. In the Cal Poly example, the leader focused on systems thinking, problem solving, team building, and information sharing. Evaluation involved assessing how well these factors were represented in the active learning environment and how well the activities supported the development and sustainability of learning. SSM-guided systems thinking, in this case, served both as the process tool for inquiry learning and, ultimately, organizational transformation (Mirijamdotter & Somerville 2008, 2009; Somerville & Howard 2008).

'Better thinking' emerged as participants experienced learning, reflected upon it (become aware of learning), and applied experiential insights to novel contexts (transferred learning). The latter proficiencies were cultivated by coaching participants through increasingly complex learning activities involving identifying and framing questions, gathering and evaluating information, organizing and synthesizing it, and presenting insights to inform and advise. Collective 'sense making', decision making, and 'action taking' activities sought to improve user experiences within the framework of the organizational strategic plan. Employee engagement evolved as co-workers learned how to solve problems, including work redesign (Hayes & Sullivan 2003) and systems design (Bødker, Kensing, & Simonsen 2004), which permitted taking advantage of new opportunities. Organizational capacity accelerated as participants learned their way to change.

References

Ackoff, R. L. (1999). *Re-creating the Corporation: A Design of Organizations for the 21st Century*. New York: Oxford University Press.

Ackoff, R. L., Magidson, J., & Addison, H. J. (2006). *Idealized Design: Creating an Organization's Future*. Philadelphia, PA: Wharton School Publishing.

Argyris, C., & Schön, D. (1991). Participatory action research and action science compared. In W. F. Whyte (ed.), *Participatory action research*. Sage Publications, Newbury Park, California, pp. 85–96.

Al-Daihani, S. M., & Rehman. S. (2007). A study of the information literacy capabilities of the Kuwaiti police officers. *The Electronic Library* 25(5): 613–626.

Barnum, Carol. (2001). *Usability Testing and Research*, New York, NY: Allyn & Bacon.

Baughman, S., & Hubbard, B. A. (2001). Becoming a learning organization. University of Maryland Libraries Working Paper #3. College Park, MD: University of Maryland. Available: http://www.lib.umd.edu/PUB/working_paper_3.html

Bechtel, Joan M. Conversation: A new paradigm for librarianship? *College & Research Libraries* 47(1986): 219–24.

Bødker, K., Kensing, F., & Simonsen, J. (2004). *Participatory IT Design: Designing for Business and Workplace Realities*. Cambridge, MA: The MIT Press.

Bruce, C. S. (1999) Workplace experiences of information literacy. *International Journal of Information Management* 19(1): 33–47.

Bennett, S. (2005). Righting the balance. In *Library as Place: Rethinking Roles, Rethinking Space*. Council on Library and Information Resources. Washington, D.C.: CLIR. Available: http://www.clir.org/pubs/reports/pub129/pub129.pdf

Bolman, L. G., & Deal, T. E. (2008). *Reframing Organizations: Artistry, Choice, and Leadership*. San Francisco, CA: Jossey-Bass.

Breivik, P. S. (2005). 21st Century learning and information literacy. *Change* 37, 20–8.

Bruce, C. S. (1997a). *The Seven Faces of Information Literacy*. Blackwood, South Australia: Auslib Press.

Bruce, C. (1997b). The relational approach: A new model for information literacy. *The New Review of Information and Library Research*, **3**, 3–22.

Bruce, C. S. (1999). Workplace experiences of information literacy. *International Journal of Information Management*, 19, 33–47.

Bruce, C. S. (2008). *Informed Learning*. Chicago: Association of College & Research Libraries.

Bundy, A. (Ed.). (2004). *Australian and New Zealand Information Literacy Framework: Principles, Standards, and Practice.* 2nd ed. Australian and New Zealand Institute for Information Literacy and Council of Australian University Librarians. Available: http://www.caul.edu.au/info-literacy/InfoLiteracyFramework.pdf

Catts, R. (2004). Preface. *Australian and New Zealand Information Literacy Framework: Principles, Standards, and Practice.* A. Bundy, ed., 2nd ed. Adelaide, Australia: Australian and New Zealand Institute for Information Literacy and Council of Australian University Librarians. Available: http://www.anziil.org/resources/Info%20lit%202nd%20edition.pdf

Checkland, P. B. (1981). *Systems Thinking, Systems Practice.* Chichester: John Wiley & Sons.

Checkland, P. B. (1985). From optimizing to learning: A development of systems thinking for the 1990s. *Journal of the Operational Research Society,* 36 (9), 757–767.

Checkland, P. B. (1994). Systems theory and management thinking. *American Behavioral Scientist,* 38 (1), 75–91.

Checkland, P. B. (1999). *Systems Thinking, Systems Practice: Includes a 30-year Retrospective.* Chichester: John Wiley & Sons.

Checkland, P. B. (2000). Soft Systems Methodology: A thirty year retrospective. *Systems Research and Behavioral Science,* 17 (S1), S11–S58.

Checkland, P. B., & Casar, A. (1986). Vickers' concept of an appreciative system: A systemic account. *Journal of Applied Systems Analysis,* 13, 3–17.

Checkland, P.B., & Holwell, S. (1998a). Action research: its nature and validity. *Systemic Practice and Action Research,* 11(1), 9–21.

Checkland, P., & Holwell, S. (1998b). *Information, Systems and Information Systems—Making Sense of the Field.* Chichester: John Wiley & Sons.

Checkland, P. B., & Poulter, J. (2006). *Learning for action. A short definitive account of soft systems methodology and its use for practitioners, teachers and students.* John Wiley & Sons, Chichester, U.K.

Checkland, P., & Scholes, J. (1990). *Soft Systems Methodology in Action.* Chichester: John Wiley & Sons.

Checkland, P. B., & Winter, M. (2006). Process and content: Two ways of using SSM. *Journal of Operational Research Society* 57, 1435–1441.

Cheuk, B. (1998a). An experienced based information literacy model in the workplace: Case studies from Singapore. In D. Booker (Ed.), *Information Literacy: The Professional Issue. Proceedings of the 3rd Australian National Information Literacy Conference* (pp. 74–82). Adelaide: University of South Australia Library.

Cheuk, B. W. (1998b). An information seeking and using process model in the workplace: A constructivist approach. *Asian Libraries* 7(12): 375–390.

Cheuk, B. W. (2000). Exploring information literacy in the workplace: A process approach. In C. Bruce and P. Candy (Eds.), *Information Literacy around the World:*

Advances in Programs and Research. Wagga Wagga, New South Wales, Center for Information Studies, Charles Sturt University, pp. 177–191.

Cheuk, B. W. (2002). Information literacy in the workplace context: Issues, best practices, and challenges. The Czech Republic, Information Literacy Meeting of Experts. Available: http://www.nclis.gov/libinter/infolitconf&meet/papers/cheuk-fullpaper.pdf

Churchman, C. W. (1971). *The Design of Inquiring Systems: Basic Concepts of Systems and Organization*. Basic Books, London, U.K.

Churchman, C. W. (1984). *The Systems Approach*. Dell Publishing Co, New York.

Cooper, Alan & Reimann, Robert. (2003). *About Face 2.0: The Essentials of Interaction Design*. Indianapolis, Indiana: Wiley Publishing.

Davis, H. L., & Somerville, M. M. (2006). Learning our way to change: Improved institutional alignment. *New Library World, 107*(3/4), 127–140.

Deiss, K. J., & Sullivan, M. (1998). The shared leadership principle: Creating leaders throughout the organization. In *Issues and Trends in Diversity, Leadership and Career Development*, D. Jones, Ed. Washington DC: Association of Research Libraries.

Dewey, B. J. (2004). The embedded librarian: Strategic campus collaborations. *Resource Sharing & Information Networks*, 17(1/2), 5–17.

Dick, B. (2004). Action research literature. Themes and trends. *Action Research*, 2(4), 425–444.

Elden, M., & Levin, M. (1991). Cogenerative learning: Bringing participation into action research. In W. F. Whyte (ed.), *Participatory action research*. Sage Publications, Newbury Park, California, pp. 127–142.

Elrod, S., & Somerville, M. M. (2007). Literature based scientific learning: A collaboration model. *Journal of Academic Librarianship, 33*(6), 684–691.

Flood, R. L. (1998). Action research and the management and systems sciences. *Systemic Practice and Action Research*, 11 (1), 79–101.

Giesecke, J. & McNeil, B. (2004). Transitioning to the learning organization. *Library Trends, 53*(1, summer), 54–67.

Gillette, D., & Somerville, M. M. (2005). Faculty and student usability and focus group findings inform Digital Teaching Library interface requirements. In *Proceedings of the 12th Annual Syllabus Higher Education Technology Conference*, Los Angeles, California.

Hayes, J., & Sullivan, M. (2003). Mapping the process: Engaging staff in work design. *Library Administration and Management*, 17 (2, Spring), 87–93.

Huysman, M., & de Wit, D. (2003). A critical evaluation of knowledge management practices. In M. S. Ackerman, V. Pipek, and V. Wulf (Eds.) *Sharing knowledge: Beyond knowledge management*, (pp. 27–55). Cambridge, MA: The MIT Press.

Jackson, M. C. (2003). *Systems Thinking: Creative Holism for Managers*. Chichester: John Wiley & Sons.

Jenlink, P.M., & Banathy, B.H. (2005). *Dialogue: conversation as culture building and consciousness evolving.* In B. Banathy & P.M. Jenlink (Eds), *Dialogue as a Means of Collective Communication*, Kluwer Academic, pp.3–14.

Krug, Steve. (2005). *Don't Make Me Think*, 2nd ed. Berkeley, CA: New Riders Publishing.

Kuhlthau, C. C. (1999). The role of experience in the information search process of an early career information worker: Perceptions of uncertainty, complexity, construction, and sources. *Journal of the American Society for Information Science*, 50 (5), 399–412.

Kuhlthau, C. C., & Tama, S. L. (2001). Information search process of lawyers: A call for 'just for me' information services. *Journal of Documentation*, 57 (1), 25–43.

Lant, P. (2001). Information literacy and teaching with technology. University of Illinois Faculty Summer Institute on Learning Technologies. Unpublished paper.

Lloyd, A. (2004). Working (in)formation: Conceptualizing information literacy in the workplace. In P. A. Danaher, C. Macpherson, F. Nouwens, & D. Orr (Eds.), *Proceedings of the 3rd International Lifelong Learning Conference*, Rockhampton, Queensland, Australia: Central Queensland University.

Lloyd, A. (2005a). No man (or woman) is an island: Information literacy, affordances, and communities of practices. *Australian Library Journal* 54(3): 230–237.

Lloyd, A. (2005b). Information literacy: Different contexts, different concepts, different truths? *Journal of Librarianship and Information Science* 37(2): 82–88.

Marton, F., & Booth, S. (1997). *Learning and Awareness.* Mahwah, NJ: Erlbaum.

Materska, K. (2004). Librarians in the knowledge age, *New Library World* 105, 142–148.

Maybee, C. (2006). Undergraduate perceptions of information use: The basis for creating user-centered student information literacy instruction. *Journal of Academic Librarianship*, 32(1), 79–85.

McIntyre, A. (2008). *Participatory Action Research. Qualitative Research Methods Series 52.* Thousand Oaks, CA: Sage Publications, Inc.

Midgley, G. (2000). *Systemic intervention: Philosophy, methodology, and practice.* New York, NY: Kluwer Academic/Plenum Publishers.

Mirijamdotter, A., & Somerville, M. M. (2005). Dynamic action inquiry: A systems approach for knowledge based organizational learning. In *Proceedings of the 11th International Conference on Human-Computer Interaction*, Las Vegas, Nevada.

Mirijamdotter, A., & Somerville, M. M. (2008). SSM inspired organizational change in a North American University Library: Lessons learned. In *Public Systems in the Future—Possibilities, Challenges, and Pitfalls: Proceedings of the 31st Information Systems Research Seminar in Scandinavia* (IRIS31), Åre, Sweden.

Mirijamdotter, A., & Somerville, M. M. (2009). Collaborative design: An SSM-enabled organizational learning approach. *International Journal of Information*

Technologies and Systems Approach 2(1), 48–69.

Morville, Peter. (2005). *Ambient Findability: What We Find Changes Who We Become.* Sebastopol, California: O'Reilly.

Norum, K. E. (2001). Appreciative design. *Systems Research and Behavioural Science* 18, 323–333.

Pan, D., Howard, Z., Somerville, M. M., & Mirijamdotter, A. (2009). From evidence to action: A shared leadership approach. Paper presented at the *5th International Evidence-Based Library and Information Practice Conference (EBLIP5)*, Stockholm, Sweden.

Pearce, C. L., & Conger, J. A. (2003). *Shared Leadership: Reframing the Hows and Whys of Leadership.* Thousand Oaks, CA: Sage Publications, Inc.

Phipps, S. (1993). Transforming libraries into learning organizations: The challenge for leadership. *Journal of Library Administration* 18, pp. 19–37.

Phipps, S. E. *(2001)*, Beyond measuring service quality: Learning from the voices of the customers, the staff, the processes, and the organization. *Library Trends*, 49, pp 635–661.

Phipps, S. (2004). The system design approach to organizational development: The University of Arizona model. *Library Trends* 53 (Summer), pp. 68–111.

Rapoport, R. (1970). Three dilemmas of action research. *Human Relations* 23: 499–513.

Rogers, E. (2005). System usability project recommendations define information architecture for library technology. In Proceedings *of the 12th Annual Syllabus Higher Education Technology Conference*, Los Angeles, California.

Rogers, E., Somerville, M. M., & Randles, A. (2005). A user-centered content architecture for an academic digital research portal. In P. Kommers & F. Richards (Eds.), *Proceedings of ED-MEDIA 2005—World Conference on Educational Multimedia, Hypermedia, & Telecommunications*, Montreal, Canada, (pp. 1172–1177). Chesapeake, Virginia: Association for the Advancement of Computing in Education.

Senge, P. M. (1990). *The Fifth Discipline: The Art and Practice of the Learning Organization.* New York: Doubleday/Currency.

Sharp, H., Rogers, Y., & Preece, J. (2007), *Interaction design: Beyond human-computer interaction, 2nd Ed.*, Wiley, England.

Smith, E. & Martina, C. (2004). Keeping the dough rising: Information in the workplace with reference to the bakery trade. In *Lifelong Learning: Whose Responsibility and What is Your Contribution?—Proceedings of the 3rd International Lifelong Learning Conference.* In P. A. Danaher, C. Macpherson, F. Nouwens, & D. Orr (Eds.), Rockhampton, Queensland, Australia: Central Queensland University. Available: http://lifelonglearning.cqu.edu.au/2004/papers

Somerville, M. M., & Brar, N. (2007). Toward co-creation of knowledge in the Interaction Age: An organizational case study. In H. K. Kaul & S. Kaul (Eds.),

Papers of the Tenth National Convention on Knowledge, Library and Information Networking (NACLIN 2007), (pp. 367–376). New Delhi, India: Developing Library Network.

Somerville, M. M., & Harlan, S. (2008), From information commons to learning commons and learning spaces: An evolutionary context, (Ed.) B. Schader, *Learning Commons: Evolution and Collaborative Essentials*. Chandos Publishing Ltd., Oxford, England, pp. 1–36.

Somerville, M. M., & Howard, Z. (2008). Systems thinking: An approach for advancing workplace information literacy. *Australian Library Journal* 57(2), 257–273.

Somerville, M. M., Huston, M. E., & Mirijamdotter, A. (2005). Building on what we know: Staff development in the digital age. *The Electronic Library* 23 (4), 480–491.

Somerville, M. M., & Mirijamdotter, A. (2005). Working smarter: An applied model for "better thinking" in dynamic information organizations. In *Currents and convergence—Navigating the rivers of change: Proceedings of the 12th National Conference of the Association of College and Research Libraries (ACRL)*, Minneapolis, Minnesota, (pp. 103–111). Chicago: Association of College and Research Libraries.

Somerville, M. M., Mirijamdotter, A., & Collins, L. (2006). Systems thinking and information literacy: Elements of a knowledge enabling workplace environment. In *Proceedings of the 39th Annual Hawaii International Conference on Systems Sciences (HICSS-39)*, Koloa, Kauai. Los Alamitos, California: IEEE Computer Society.

Somerville, M. M., & Schader, B. (2005). Life after the reference desk: Co-creating a digital age library. *The Charleston Advisor* 7(1), 56–57.

Somerville, M. M., Schader, B., & Huston, M. E. (2005). Rethinking what we do and how we do it: Systems thinking strategies for library leadership. *Australian Academic and Research Libraries* 36(4), 214–227.

Somerville, M. M., & Vazquez, F. V. (2004). Constructivist workplace learning: An idealized design project. *Proceedings of the 3rd International Lifelong Learning Conference* (pp. 300–305 plus errata page). Rockhampton, Australia: Central Queensland University.

Somerville, M. M., & Vuotto, F. (2005). If you build it with them, they will come: Digital research portal design and development strategies. *Internet Reference Services Quarterly: A Journal of Innovative Information Practice, Technologies, and Resources* 10(1), 77–94.

Stacey, R. (2003). Learning as an activity of interdependent people. *The Learning Organization* 10 (6), 325–331.

Stacey, R. D. (2004). *Complex responsive processes in organizations: Learning and knowledge creation*. London: Routledge.

Susman, G., & Evered, R. (1978). An assessment of the scientific merits of action research. *Administrative Science Quarterly* 23 (4), 582–603.

Varey, R. J. (2005). Informational and communicational explanations of corporations as interaction systems. In M. Wiberg (Ed.), *The Interaction Society: Practice, Theories and Supportive Technologies*, (pp. 139–170). Hershey, PA: Information Science Publishing.

Vickers, G. (1983a). *The Art of Judgment. A Study of Policy Making*. London: Harper & Row Ltd.

Vickers, G. (1983b). *Human Systems Are Different*. London: Harper & Row Ltd.

Whyte, W. F., Greenwood, D. J., & Lazes, P. (1991). Participatory action research through practice to science in social research. In W. F. Whyte (Ed.), *Participatory Action Research*, (pp. 19–55). Newbury Park, CA: Sage Publications.

Wilson, B. (2001). *Soft Systems Methodology: Conceptual Model Building and its Contribution*. Chichester: John Wiley & Sons.

Chapter Six
Working Together Essentials

Contemporary library organizations exist amidst dynamically changing internal and external circumstances. Precipitated by accelerating change, increasing uncertainty, growing ambiguity, and heightened complexity, these unrelenting forces demand significant organizational development (Sullivan 2004a, 2004b, 1991). In response, this concluding chapter distills essential elements for collaborative creation of an organizational learning environment which enables 'forward thinking' direction setting, decision making, and action planning. These concepts emerged as 'working together' essentials in the California Polytechnic State University experiences. They have since served as guiding principles for developing vibrant learning communities in the libraries at San José State University and the University of Colorado Denver. These elements are presented and discussed here with generous references to core literature for organizations seeking to customize these concepts to local conditions and circumstances … whether in Paris, France or Paris, Texas.

Information, action, and outcomes oriented, this organizational learning approach aims to use a variety of means to incrementally build collective staff capacity for working together through asking good questions, selecting authoritative sources, creating relevant interpretations, organizing emerging insights, and communicating them to inform, educate, and influence. By virtue of both its content and also its process, these collaborative information practices are therefore especially suitable for libraries and other information and knowledge organizations.

The action research origins ensure that while workplace inquiry serves to explore, engage, and extend relationships among people and ideas, projects also aim to simultaneously bring improvements in a situation while learning from the process of deriving the change. Collaborative discovery strategies, therefore, employ learning activities 'with and for' organizational beneficiaries to continuously improve user experiences. Over time and with practice, robust information exchange and knowledge creation practices enlarge consultation circles and deepen inquiry relationships. Workplace culture becomes enriched by purposeful communication, dialogue, and reflection practices. Through an ongoing interplay of action, observation, and evaluation, nimble responsiveness is enabled and animated—initiating never-ending individual, team, and organizational learning aimed at ever-deepening insight and performance.

Learning Organization Fundamentals
In 1990, Dr. Peter Senge advanced the notion of a 'learning organization' in

his groundbreaking book, *The Fifth Discipline.* In this volume, he identifies five disciplines necessary for 'generative learning': systems thinking, personal mastery, mental models, shared vision, and team learning. The five disciplines can be approached at one of three levels: practices (what you do), principles (guiding ideas and insights), and essences (the state of being for those with high levels of disciplinary mastery).

When these series of principles and practices are studied, mastered, and integrated, a shift of mind occurs—moving people "from seeing parts to seeing wholes, from seeing people as helpless reactors to seeing them as active participants in shaping their reality, from reacting to the present to creating the future" (Senge 1990, 69). The conceptual cornerstone of the learning organization, then, is the fifth discipline—systems thinking. Its theory and practice avoids the common mistake of focusing on the parts rather than seeing the whole or, correspondingly, failing to see the organization as a dynamic process. Stated positively, a better appreciation of systems can lead to more appropriate actions.

Each discipline, however, is necessary for the organization to learn. For instance, mental models are "deeply engrained assumptions, generalizations, or even pictures or images that influence how we understand the world and how we take action" (ibid. 8). Donald A. Schön (1983) referred to this as professional 'repertoire' for a reflective practitioner. Because people tend to be unaware of the impact of implicit assumptions on their behavior, a fundamental responsibility for professionals is—in Schön's terms—to develop the ability to reflect-in- and –on-action. "It also includes the ability to carry on 'learningful' conversations that balance inquiry and advocacy, where people expose their own thinking effectively and make that thinking open to the influence of others" (Senge 1990, 9). This 'dialogue-enabling' capability is important because "entrenched mental models ... thwart changes that could come from systems thinking" (ibid. 203).

When organizations can transcend limiting mental models and embrace systems thinking, it is possible to bring shared vision to fruition. "The practice of shared vision involves the skills of unearthing shared 'pictures of the future' that foster genuine commitment and enrollment rather than compliance" (ibid. 9). This quite naturally occurs because "as people talk, the vision grows clearer. As it gets clearer, enthusiasm for its benefits grow" (ibid. 227).

Personal mastery requires continually clarifying and deepening personal vision, focusing individual energies and insights, and developing persistence and patience. "People with a high level of personal mastery live in a continual learning mode" (ibid. 142) and, although individual learning does not guarantee organizational learning, "without it no organization learns" (ibid. 139).

The final discipline is team learning, "the process of aligning and developing the capabilities of a team to create the results its members truly desire" (ibid.

227). It builds on personal mastery and shared vision—but these elements are not enough. People need to be able to act together. "The discipline of team learning starts with 'dialogue', the capacity of members of a team to suspend assumptions and enter into a genuine 'thinking together'. To the Greeks *dialogos* meant a free-flowing of meaning through a group, allowing the group to discover insights not attainable individually" (ibid. 10). In combination with systems thinking, collective thought processes can productively explore and improve deep-seated structural issues and forces.

It naturally follows that learning organizations require appropriate leadership. Senge sees the traditional view of leaders—as special people who set the directions and make key decisions—as deriving from a deeply individualistic and non-systemic worldview. Fundamentally, this premise "is based on assumptions of people's powerlessness, their lack of personal vision and inability to master the forces of change, deficits which can be remedied only by a few great leaders" (ibid. 340). In challenging this traditional view, Senge proposes that leaders in a learning organization are designers, stewards, and teachers responsible for building organizations where people continually expand their capabilities to understand complexity, clarify vision, and share models.

In designing an organizational learning environment, leaders ensure that people throughout the organization can productively anticipate and address critical issues through exercising the five disciplines. To accomplish this, leaders ensure that an invisible architecture provides a 'container' which supports the reflection and dialogue necessary for generative learning. When workplace policies, procedures, and systems ensure a "setting in which the intensities of human activity can safely emerge" (Isaacs 1999, 242), people are able to move beyond patterns of meaning dominated by memory, thereby liberating a process of movement toward realization of the creative self (Bohm 1992).

In discussing the notion of leader as steward, Senge recalls the prevalence of 'purpose stories' in his interviews with corporate managers. These "overarching explanation of why they do what they do, how their organization needs to evolve, and how that evolution is part of something larger" (Senge 1990, 346) offer a single set of integrated ideas that give meaning to and vision for the leaders' work. However, Senge notes, leaders do not own the vision. Rather, they are responsible for shaping it for the benefit of others—'choosing service over self-interest' in the words of Peter Block (1993). In telling stories, then, leaders both advance shared vision and invite others' involvement, using language to change how people work (Kegan & Lahey 2001).

Given leaders' learning responsibilities, Senge underscores the importance of the teacher role, noting that "much of the leverage leaders can actually exert lies in helping people achieve more accurate, more insightful and more *empowering* views of reality" (1990, 353). "'Leader as teacher' is not about 'teaching' people how to achieve their vision. It is about fostering learning, for everyone" (ibid. 356). This depends on simultaneously attending to four ways of influencing people's reality: significant events, behavioral patterns, systemic structures, and purpose stories. While leaders in learning organization focus on all four levels, they are especially mindful of furthering 'big picture' understanding of organizational purpose and systemic structure—and they 'teach' people throughout the organization to do likewise. This allows everyone to achieve enterprise views and appreciate structural conditions that create the conditions conducive to successful workplace behaviors (Hughes & Beatty 2005). By attending to such high-level purposes, a concept that remains open to challenge and further improvement, leaders cultivate collective awareness of what the organization and its members can become.

Communities of Practice

Within such a learning framework, organizations are most appropriately envisioned as communities where knowledge, identity, and learning are situated. This framework acknowledges the social context of learning—i.e., that knowledge is acquired and understood through action, interaction, and sharing with others (Duguid 2005). It follows that social networks provide peer-to-peer enculturation through intentional exchange of tacit information made explicit. This, in turn, enables a dynamic process experienced as a continuous spiral that perpetually elevates collective understanding and enables knowledge creation (Nonaka, Konno, & Toyama 2000).

Building knowledge production capability within an organization therefore relies on development and implementation of appropriate, flexible organizational environments that foster robust exchange relationships and effective collaborations (von Kough, Ichijo, & Nonaka 2000). This organizational design concept recognizes the need for cultivating both formal and informal interactions among individuals and with information to enable knowledge creation and advance workplace learning.

In turn, the communal nature of learning predicts the importance of creating organizational environments where knowledge arises out of processes that are personal, social, situated and active. It follows that workplaces must provide both formal and informal learning opportunities for interaction with ideas and among individuals. Through complementary organizational processes, "meaning making" is negotiated in formal face-to-face meetings supplemented by informal dialogue. Sustainable outcomes depend on boundary crossing relationships fortified by formal and informal information exchanges aimed at advancing collective learning.

This organizational learning framework integrates Wenger's notions of communities of practice, Nonaka's theories on knowledge creation, and Bruce's framework of workplace information fluency. It assumes, as the Cal Poly examples illustrates, that organizational capacity is fuelled by information encounters experienced within ever expanding workplace contexts. Toward that end, workplace redesign should purposefully foster contextualizing information interactions to advance knowledge sharing and further community building. Success indicators must acknowledge that a primary source of value creation lies in social processes which are oftentimes informal, that build learning communities and foster knowledge production. Such social relationships can activate and perpetuate organizational learning and, thereby, cultivate knowledge creation over time through human interactions (Griffin 2002, Stacey 2004, Jakubik 2008) within social networks in communities of practice (Wenger & Synder 2000).

A knowledge-enabling environment, therefore, refers to the organizational structures that create opportunities for learning through providing conditions conducive to working together. This context-setting infrastructure enables knowledge creation, "an intensely human, messy process of imagination, invention and learning from mistakes, embedded in a web of human relationships" (Senge & Scharmer 2001, 247). An organizational knowledge vision must recognize the critical importance of enabling appropriately contextualized formal and informal interactions with ideas and among individuals. The resulting dialogues depend upon a deep and broad appreciation for and engagement with tacit knowledge made explicit (Nonaka 1994). Often, these efforts benefit from mobilizing 'knowledge activists' who serve as 'thought leaders' and 'culture shapers' (Somerville & Howard 2008). As 'boundary spanners,' they further globalization—throughout the organization—of local knowledge (Howard & Somerville 2008). Additionally, because organizational learning benefits from a workplace that is appropriately flexible, future oriented, and intrinsically fulfilling (von Krogh, Ichijo, & Nonaka 2000), learning outcomes must ultimately enhance the multidimensional elements of knowledge creation.

Knowledge-Enabling Essentials

Notions about community building for organizational learning and, ultimately, knowledge creation provide the fundamental underpinnings for a contemporary workplace learning environment. As explained by Nonaka (1994), knowledge creation is activated and sustained by the continuous social interaction of tacit and explicit knowledge through a four phase spiral process. The sequential modes of catalytic knowledge conversion involve socialization, externalization, combination and internalization, before returning once more—in an iterative fashion—to socialization (Gourlay 2006). Nonaka's notion of *ba*, a shared space for developing collegial relationships and creating knowledge, conceptualizes the ideal, persistent workplace learning environment. Within this space—which may be physical, virtual, mental, or a combination, a collective "transcendental perspective can emerge which integrates information into knowledge, within a context that harbors meaning" (Nonaka 1994). This 'sense making' is necessarily social in nature, animated by dynamic, iterative 'perspective taking' and 'perspective making' processes (Boland & Tenkasi 1995) through which people assign meaning and construct reality (Berger & Luckmann 1967)

When Nonaka's findings about the elements and forces within a knowledge enabling environment are coupled with insights from Wenger and Snyder's social learning systems research on communities of practice, a powerful and practical framework emerges for advancing organizational learning and developing knowledge capabilities. Within this context, an organization can be conceptualized as a purposeful social interaction system (Checkland & Holwell 1998) in which collective capabilities develop through workplace socialization processes (Lloyd 2004). An organization's knowledge vision, then, must recognize the importance of establishing sustainable organizational structures and communication systems that encourage and enable the social interactions which promote investigation and negotiation of the interests, judgments, and decisions through which people learn interdependently (Stacey 2003, 2004). In this context, 'culture' serves as a shared basis of appreciation and action developed through communication within an organizational system (Checkland 1994, Jenlink & Banathy 2005).

It naturally follows that through ever expanding boundaries of influence and engagement, a workplace learning environment serves as the arena in which knowledge develops through 'meaningful' encounters that activate prior understanding within individuals and among groups. As co-workers listen to different interpretations and process them together, "the information becomes amplified. In this process of shared reflection, a small finding can grow as it feeds back on itself, building in significance with each new perception or interpretation.... the simple process of iteration eventually reveals the complexity hidden within the issue. From this level of understanding, creative responses emerge and significant change becomes possible" (Wheatley 1994, 115). The synergy that emerges from making connections between and among ideas and individuals recognizes that development of workplace information literacy also depends on shared purpose sufficient to facilitate the 'intersubjective' making of meaning. This 'interpersonal glue' among organizational members occurs through the exchange of information and insights, a complex process consisting of 'perspective making' and 'perspective taking' which, in time, develops the collegial trust and caring necessary to moving beyond information hoarding to advance information sharing. When fortified by an action research orientation, these workplace elements can bring about change in the situation while learning from the process of deriving change. Furthering organizational learning and advancing stakeholder relationships holds promise for avoiding an 'inward looking' library centric orientation while encouraging sustained 'outward looking' and outcomes oriented learning and improved anticipation of users' changing needs.

This approach departs substantively from past practices that relied on counting 'busy-ness' data—e.g., circulation statistics, reference transactions, and instructional sessions. In contrast, an 'outcomes oriented' approach is driven by user generated issues, questions, and aspirations. A combination of methodologies, including online surveys, focus groups, and usability studies, can develop an accurate composite of users. Based on listening to the voices of diverse library constituencies, staff members improve their understanding of service and program expectations. They experience efficacy when evaluating current approaches and imagining potential improvements. As dialogue feeds and informs deep relearning, conversations continue to inform 'what we change and how we change', as better ways of leading, learning, reflecting, and working evolve through formal and informal teaching, coaching, and mentoring.

Throughout, information resources animate the learning potential of information encounters (Bruce 1999, 2008) contextualized through continuous reflection and dialogue processes (Callahan & Howard 2008) that fuel the creation and integration of collective organizational understanding. Iterative in nature, the cyclical process naturally heightens both depth and breadth of knowledge among individuals and groups when situated within a purposeful organizational learning environment. In this way, texturized, workplace information encounters—in a spiraling fashion—ensure that learning emerges out of a growing knowledge base. This process naturally leads to the creation and integration of new knowledge, even as it guarantees perpetual (and multi-perspectival) knowledge flow—which ultimately leads to knowledge creation and transfer through the continuous interaction of explicit and tacit knowledge.

The essence of this catalytic process—whereby information instigates learning—depends on Bruce's theoretical model which recognizes that organizational learning involves experiential relationships with topics and relational thinking (Somerville & Howard 2008). Such a 'constellation of skills, practices and processes' (Lloyd 2006) serves to connect information sources in the workplace with the transferable learning practices required to access them, thereby facilitating the conversion from individual to collective views of practices and competencies, as well as integration within situated inquiry-based contexts (Lloyd 2005a, 2005b).

This line of thinking applies a social constructivist learning approach to describe the workings of a community of practice (Wenger, McDermott, & Snyder

2002), as "informally bound together by shared expertise and passion for the joint enterprise" (Wenger & Synder 2000, 139). Within such a group, knowledge and experiences are openly shared to foster new ideas and approaches to problems. In other words, a community of practice exists to produce shared (better) practices as members engage in the collective process of learning through interacting within a social context (Wenger 1998). Knowledge, therefore, is embedded in human relations fostered when individuals interact within a 'sense making' social context (Jakubik 2008). In this way, communities of practice are self organizing and self perpetuating: as they generate knowledge, they reinforce and renew themselves.

Communities of practice fulfill a number of functions with respect to the creation, accumulation, and diffusion of knowledge in an organization. They operate as 'culture shapers' when they continue to exchange, interpret and build information to create knowledge. They serve as 'boundary bridgers' when they share knowledge beyond the constructs of particular communities of practice. They also fulfill 'thought leadership' roles as they retain and enhance knowledge through dynamic, living ways that also steward workplace competencies to keep the organization at the cutting edge. In addition, communities of practice provide individuals with an identity within the workplace, which ensures a professional and/or disciplinary lens through which to perceive and inquire. This offers a vantage point from which to develop trans-disciplinary and cross functional workplace understanding.

Knowledge Enabling Elements

In identifying essential organizational learning components, Wenger (1998) identifies the need to build organizational environments that recognize, support, and leverage the capacity for communities of practice to create, retain, and harness organizational knowledge. This framework includes designing organizational structures and processes to give primacy to informal learning processes, placing emphasis on meaningful organizational participation and community membership, and organizing the complexity of workplace communities to enable easy access to local knowledge (Wenger 2000).

In addition, 21st century knowledge-enabling technologies can foster organizational effectiveness by allowing participants in communities of practice to share, converse, and create across time and space. In supplementing face-to-face interactions, appropriate technology can ensure that "the knowledge of each individual who is part of the group is shared beyond temporal, spatial or structural limits" (Sarabia 2007). The widespread availability of Web 2.0 tools can especially accelerate communication, discussion and information sharing, allowing the local experience of the individual or team to be shared across the whole organization.

This approach is especially effective when paired with a learning framework that acknowledges the catalytic effect of information encounters within enabling contexts.

The resulting 'informed learning' (Bruce 2008) pairs disciplinary mastery with information literacy and workplace performance (Goad 2002). Such an approach recognizes that for potential learning to occur, information encounters must be experienced as sufficiently relevant to activate and extend prior understanding. Additionally, workplace circumstances must encourage reflection at both an individual and collective level, and dialogue must promote engagement with information for learning transferable to novel circumstances (Pan, Howard, Somerville, & Mirijamdotter 2009).

At its essence, informed learning furthers the simultaneous development of discipline and process learning. In accomplishing this within an information or knowledge organization environment, leaders must appreciate how staff members are experiencing both information use and also information content. These insights can then be intentionally furthered through workplace information experiences. Then, as staff members experience the efficacy of information experience and usage as empowering, they will evolve an understanding of its practical application in furthering organizational purposes—i.e., they will see informed learning as a process that should transform both learning and the culture of communities for the better (Breivik 2000).

Informed learning, therefore, is about the recognition that new learning experiences lead to understanding the world in new or more complex ways (Marton & Booth 1997). It follows then that 'working smarter' (Somerville, Howard, & Mirijamdotter 2009) as an information or knowledge worker requires 'making sense' of increasingly more complex information experiences. From the library and information science perspective, this may be expressed through heightened understanding of particular aspects of the professional field. From the information use position, this may be expressed through diversified experiences of information practices in terms which extend the depth and breadth of the information universe (Bruce, Edwards, & Lupton 2006).

From a holistic viewpoint, informed learning can be understood as a cyclical process of acquiring information for the purpose of using information for learning (Lupton 2008). Within the realm of professional information practices, this might be expressed by managers as a need for "getting information in, manipulating it, getting it out" (Bruce 2008, 94) and involve a variety of means ranging from standard text-based reports to Web 2.0 enabled communication systems (Howard & Somerville 2008, Somerville & Yusko 2008). Over time and with practice, managers develop professional efficacy which, in turn, advances organizational effectiveness, even as they learn how to learn and how to cultivate that in others. Increasing, this is demonstrated through 'evidence based' (Partridge, Thorpe, & Edwards 2007) decision making, in which rich workplace dialogue explores what constitutes authoritative evidence within particular subspecialties of the field.

In a highly complementary fashion, Australian researcher Lloyd has offered a rich conception of the workplace environment which characterizes the interactive nature of 'working together' in contemporary information and knowledge organizations. In amplifying Bruce's theories, Lloyd's research-generated findings suggest that informed learning involves collaborative, socio-cultural practices within a context specific environment (Lloyd 2004, Lloyd 2005b). Consisting of a constellation of skills, practices and processes (Lloyd 2006), these collaborative information practices further the construction of shared professional meanings and the development of collective outcomes through situated engagement with information. These contextualizing experiences inform the creation of experiential conceptions (Bruce, Edwards, & Lupton 2006) with transformative implications. This includes the use of diverse lenses (Kreitz 2008) to view information and knowledge production, which potentially challenges existing social practices and power relationships; questions implicit and explicit assumptions and meanings; examines stakeholders' agendas and relative privileges; and reflects upon what constitutes knowledge and authority (Bruce 2008).

The transformative power of informed workplace learning is that, at its very essence, it is collectively experienced at both group and organizational levels through substantive engagement with the four key sources of workplace learning (Billett 1999): the activities of work, the workplace, other workers, and the practices of listening and observing. In extending this notion, Lloyd (2005a) recognizes that the development of workplace proficiencies require context specific learning processes that connect information sources in the workplace with the learning practices required to activate them. The close correspondence between information experience facets and common workplace activities (Bruce 1999) suggests the necessity of making learning explicit within professional practice experiences of both individuals and organizations.

Organizational Learning Framework

In developing a workplace learning framework, participatory design principles can be successfully combined with reflective information practices to cultivate informed employees who are engaged, enabled, and enriched by the social, procedural, and physical information that constitutes their information universe. To accomplish this, purposeful socialization processes and workplace contexts must be available to facilitate meaningful workplace information encounters. Time and practice can evolve collaborative inquiry processes, fostered largely by informal workplace social relationships that encourage engagement with and draw meaning from social and physical information sources as well as from textual knowledge sources (Lloyd 2006). In this way, new ideas surface through everyday social interactions with colleagues (Kirk 2004) when co-workers begin to *use information to learn* (Bruce 2008).

Within this context, an organization is conceptualized as a purposeful social interaction system (Checkland & Holwell 1998) in which collective capabilities develop through workplace socialization processes (Lloyd 2005a). An organization's 'knowledge vision' (von Krogh, Ichijo, & Nonaka 2000), then, must recognize the importance of establishing a sustainable organizational environment that encourages and enables social interactions and promotes investigation and negotiation of the interests, judgments, and decisions through which people learn interdependently (Stacey 2003). It naturally follows that workplace 'culture' serves as a shared basis of appreciation and action developed through organizational communication (Jenlink &Banathy 2005).

In such a workplace learning environment, knowledge emerges through encounters perceived as meaningful which activate prior understanding to produce improved 'sense making' within individuals and among groups. To animate learning, information encounters must be adequately situated and purposefully guided. Workplace learning activities must be information-centered, learning-focused, and action-oriented. Over time and with practice, an evolutionary organizational culture will enable and sustain knowledge creation

The essence of this catalytic process—whereby information instigates learning—depends on cultivating experiential relationships with topics and surfacing relational thinking about ideas (Somerville & Howard 2008). Such a "constellation of skills, practices and processes" (Lloyd 2006) serves to connect information sources in the workplace with the transferable learning practices required to access them, thereby facilitating the conversion from individual to collective capacity for practices and competencies. These proficiencies include asking good questions, selecting authoritative sources, evaluating multiple perspectives, organizing emerging insights, and communicating them to inform, educate, and influence. This intentional learning focus anticipates contemporary organizations' urgent need to survive volatile internal and external changes through informed and agile responsiveness.

Organizational Leadership Elements

Ultimately, responsibility for creation of a robust organizational environment to activate and accelerate learning resides with organizational leaders (Belasen 2000). They must be mindful that the five disciplines which undergird a learning organization must be practiced—i.e., these disciplines cannot be learned and achieved without practice over time. They must also appreciate and demonstrate that the five disciplines are inherently interrelated, as suggested below:

- Personal Mastery requires learning to expand our personal capacity to create the results we most desire, and creating an organizational environment which encourages all its members to develop themselves toward the goals they choose.

- Mental Models involves reflecting upon, continually clarifying, and improving our internal pictures of the world, and seeing how they shape our actions and decisions. Mental models are the assumptions and stories we carry with us about others and ourselves. Mental models help us function but do not always correlate with reality.

- Shared Vision necessitates building a sense of commitment in a group, by developing shared images of the future we seek to create, and the principles and guiding practices by which we hope to get there. Everyone contributes to the shared vision. Creating a vision is an evolutionary process.

- Team Learning encompasses transforming conversational and collective thinking skills, so that groups of people can reliably develop intelligence and ability greater than the sum of individual members' talents. This is our collective capacity to do something. In team learning there is less authority and more emphasis on collaboration and facilitation. There is a great deal of trust among and between members.

- Systems Thinking becomes a way of thinking about, and a language for describing and understanding, the forces and interrelationships that shape the behavior of systems. This discipline helps us see how to change systems more effectively, and to act more in tune with the larger processes of the natural and economic world. Systems thinking serves as the cornerstone for the other disciplines (Baughman & Hubbard 2001).

Firsthand experience learning about these disciplines through a variety of workplace situations will further library staff members' understanding of themselves and the organization. With that comes recognition of the important connection between who they are as individuals and the organization's effectiveness and success (Shaughnessy 1995). In a shared leadership environment, these personal attributes become critically important characteristics of 'followers' too (Deiss & Sullivan 1998). As workplace assumptions and resultant relationships for working together evolve, organization members collaboratively create their organizational future. To achieve this, leaders must ensure collaborative design processes that activate continuous learning cycles, whereby participants identify opportunities and formulate questions, find and appraise information, and then apply insightful interpretations to achieve meaningful performance outcomes. Because such (re) thinking is circular rather than linear, the search for solutions requires devising iterative, perpetual learning processes which cross traditional departmental and divisional boundaries. Continuous learning also requires considering multiple viewpoints which encourage seeing the organization for what it is: a complex organism affected by factors within and without. Reaching this understanding—and then activating and maintaining it in the form of research-in-practice—requires enriching the workplace environment with ongoing activities which are information-centered and action-oriented. To achieve this, organizational leaders must fulfill essential responsibilities, including these:

- Design of workplace systems and structures which facilitate information access, information exchange, and reflective dialogue,
- Advancement of collaborative relationships which accelerate learning in house and on campus,
- Allocation of human and financial resources to incentivize collective innovation and creativity, and
- Co-creation of a collaborative design, implementation, and assessment culture with campus stakeholders (Somerville 2008).

Throughout, organizational leaders foster and sustain workplace socialization and learning processes to support informed learning, using information-centered experiences to cultivate new ways of understanding. With practice, workplace capabilities are enhanced through meaningful encounters within the social, procedural and physical information environments. In time, organizational culture is transformed from reactive to proactive, enabled by rich relational information experiences and social interaction opportunities among workplace participants and organizational beneficiaries.

Transferable Learning Insights

The quintessential elements for ensuring robust organizational processes, purposes, and relationships involve initiating dialogue, creating meaning, forming intentions, and taking action. These activities require an appreciative setting created by leaders who ensure enabling learning experiences in which individuals exercise powerful inquiry tools and reflective practices to 'learn the way' *for and with* present and potential library beneficiaries.

These knowledge-driven processes in turn inform collaborative information practices for initiating and sustaining the socialization that enables effective information practices and advances workplace learning. As collective context grows, it guides iterative processes for evaluating meaningful data, comparing and contrasting multiple interpretations, infusing reflective insights, and pursuing unsolved curiosities, into a continuous learning process that challenges existing ways of seeing and doing. When this occurs, it also informs co-creation of organization futures characterized by nimble responsiveness.

In traditional organizations, this invention process for generating 'ideal futures' requires rethinking organizational structure, service priorities, and staff assignments, guided by organizational leaders who foster the application and advancement of information literacy, knowledge generation, and collaborative learning. Through revisiting and re-inventing professional roles, campus relationships, and library institutions defined by industrial age models, librarians move from traditional information gatekeeper functions to fulfill rewarding new knowledge age roles.

This holistic organizational learning framework can overtly guide participants' performance of day-to-day workplace activities as they relearn how to engage with information, coworkers, stakeholders, and users. As their new roles begin to extend well beyond the boundaries of library units and library walls, employees exercise new language and tools for discussing and analyzing complexities and interdependencies within an extended universe of organizational influence and possibility.

Construction of such a workplace environment, fortified by enabling learning systems and work processes, requires engaged and dedicated employees with the disposition and tools to study, master, and integrate five sets of disciplinary principles and practices into their working lives. In addition, they must learn to respect and engage others' ideas, behaviors, and beliefs in order to enjoy convivial and creative workplace experiences that advance a common purpose. As the whole system is understood, accountability becomes fully distributed, performance gaps are quickly identified and addressed, improving productivity and customer satisfaction. Creativity is sparked as people from all levels of the organization contribute their best ideas, thereby increasing capacity for future changes as people develop the skills and processes to meet current and future challenges (Axelrod 2002).

Over time and with practice, as these collective conditions develop, organizational capacity ensures nimble responsiveness to dynamic and unprecedented circumstances, prompting participants to become both reflective (re)learners and also responsive action takers. In addition, a collaborative learning environment ensures that practical problem solving occurs simultaneous with professional enrichment as employees reconsider organizational purposes, reinvent constituency relationships, and re-imagine workplace roles within the larger academic enterprise.

References

Axelrod, R. H. (2002). *Terms of Engagement: Changing the Way We Change Organizations*. San Francisco, CA: Berrett-Koehler Publishers.

Baughman, S., & Hubbard, B. A. (2001). *Becoming a learning organization*. University of Maryland Libraries Working Paper #3. College Park, MD: University of Maryland. Available: http://www.lib.umd.edu/PUB/working_paper_3.html

Belasen, A. T. (2000). *Leading the Learning Organization: Communication and Competencies for Managing Change*. New York: State University of New York Press.

Berger, P. L, & Luckmann, T. (1967). *The Social Construction of Reality: A Treatise in the Sociology of Knowledge*. Garden City, NY: Doubleday.

Billett, S. (1999). Guided learning in the workplace. In D. Boud and J Garrick (Eds). *Understanding Learning at Work*. London: Routledge.

Block, P. (1993). *Stewardship: Choosing Service Over Self-Interest*. San Francisco: Berrett-Koehler.

Bohm, D. (1992). *Thought as a System*. London: Routledge.

Boland, R., & Tenkasi, R. (1995) Perspective making and perspective taking in communities of knowing. *Organization Science*, 6(4), 350–372.

Breivik, P. (2000). Foreword. In C. Bruce & P. Candy (Eds.), *Information Literacy Around the World: Advances in Programs and Research* (p. xi). Riverina, New South Wales, Australia: Centre for Information Studies, Charles Sturt University.

Bruce, C. (1999). Workplace experiences of information literacy. *International Journal of Information Management*, 19, 33–47.

Bruce, C. S. (2008). *Informed Learning*. Chicago, IL: Association of College and Research Libraries.

Bruce, C. Edwards, S., & Lupton, M. (2006). Six frames for information literacy education: a conceptual framework for interpreting the relationships between theory and practice, *Innovations in Teaching and Learning Information and Computer Science*, 5(1). Available: http://www.ics.heacademy.ac.uk/italics/vol5-1/pdf/six-frames_final%20_1_.pdf

Callahan, A., & Howard, Z. (2008). Planning for success: Reprioritising, repurposing and retooling with results. *Proceedings of 5th International Lifelong Learning Conference: Reflecting on successes and framing futures, pp.* 85–90. Rockhampton, Queensland: Central Queensland University.

Checkland, P.B. (1994). Systems theory and management thinking. *American Behavioral Scientist*, 38(1), 75–91.

Checkland, P., & Holwell, S. (1998). *Information, Systems and Information Systems— Making Sense of the Field*. Chichester: John Wiley & Sons.

Deiss, K. J., & Sullivan, M. (1998). The shared leadership principle: Creating leaders throughout the organization. In *Issues and Trends in Diversity, Leadership and Career Development*, D. Jones, Ed. Washington DC: Association of Research Libraries.

Duguid, Paul. (2005). The Art of Knowing: Social and Tacit Dimensions of Knowledge and the Limits of the Community of Practice. *The Information Society*, 21, 109–118.

Goad, T. (2002). *Information Literacy and Workplace Performance*. Westport, CT: Quorum Books.

Gourlay, S. (2006). Conceptualizing knowledge creation: A critique of Nonaka's theory. *Journal of Management Studies*, 43(7), 1415–1436.

Griffin, D. (2002). *The Emergence of Leadership: Linking Self-Organization and Ethics*. London: Routledge.

Howard, Z., & Somerville, M. M. (2008). Building knowledge capabilities: An organisational learning approach. In *Harnessing Knowledge Management to Build Communities—Proceedings of the 11ᵗʰ Annual Conference on Knowledge Management and Intelligent Decision Support* (ACKMIDS08), Ballarat, Victoria, Australia.

Hughes, R. L., & Beatty, K. C. (2005). *Becoming a Strategic Leader—Your Role in Your Organization's Enduring Success*. San Francisco, CA: Jossey-Bass.

Isaacs, W. (1999). *Dialogue and the Art of Thinking Together: A Pioneering Approach to Communicating in Business and in Life*. New York: Currency.

Jakubik, M. (2008). Experiencing collaborative knowledge creation processes. *The Learning Organization*, 15(1), 5–25.

Jenlink, P.M. & Banathy, B.H. (2005). Dialogue: conversation as culture building and consciousness evolving. In B. Banathy & P.M. Jenlink (Eds), *Dialogue as a Means of Collective Communication*, Kluwer Academic, pp.3–14.

Kegan, R., & Lahey, L. L. (2001). *How the Way We Talk Can Change the Way We Work: Seven Languages for Transformation*. San Francisco, CA: Jossey-Bass.

Kirk, J. (2004). Information and work: Extending the roles of information professionals. *Challenging Ideas—Proceedings of the ALIA 2004 Biennial Conference*, pp. 21–24. Kingston, Australia: Australia Library and Information Association.

Kreitz, P. (2008). Best practices for managing organizational diversity. *Journal of Academic Librarianship* 34(2, March): 101–120.

Lloyd, A. (2004). Working (in)formation: conceptualizing information literacy in the workplace, *Lifelong learning: whose responsibility and what is your contribution? Refereed papers from the 3rd International Lifelong Learning Conference*, pp. 218–224. Rockhampton, Queensland, Australia: Central Queensland University Press.

Lloyd, A. (2005a). No man (or woman) is an island: information literacy, affordances, and communities of practices, *Australian Library Journal*, vol. 54 no. 3, pp. 230–237.

Lloyd, A. (2005b). Information literacy: different contexts, different concepts, different truths?, *Journal of Librarianship and Information Science*, vol. 37 no.2, pp. 82–88.

Lloyd, A. (2006). Information literacy landscapes: an emerging picture, *Journal of Documentation*, 62(5), 570–583.

Lupton, M. (2008). Information literacy and learning. PhD dissertation. Brisbane, Australia: Queensland University of Technology. Available: http://adt.library.qut.edu.au

Marton, F. & Booth, S. (1997). *Learning and Awareness*. Mahwah, NJ: Erlbaum.

Mirijamdotter, M., & Somerville, M. M. (2009). Collaborative design: An SSM-enabled organizational learning approach. *International Journal of Information Technologies and Systems Approach*, 2(1), 48–69.

Nonaka, I. (1994). A dynamic theory of organizational knowledge creation. *Organization Science*, 5(1), 14–37.

Nonaka, I., Konno, N., & Toyama, R. (2000). SECI, *Ba* and leadership: A unified model of dynamic knowledge creation. *Long Range Planning*, 33, 5–34.

Pan, D., Howard, Z., Somerville, M. M., & Mirijamdotter, A. (2009). From evidence to action: A shared leadership approach. Paper presented at the 5th *International Evidence-Based Library and Information Practice Conference (EBLIP5)*, Stockholm, Sweden.

Partridge, H., Thorpe, C., & Edwards, S. L. (2007). The practitioner's experience and conception of library and information based practice: An exploratory analysis. Paper presented at the 4th International Library and Information Practice Based Conference, Chapel Hill-Durham, North Carolina. Available: http://www.eblip4.unc.edu/papers/Partridge.pdf

Sarabia, M. (2007). Knowledge leadership cycles: an approach from Nonaka's viewpoint. *Journal of Knowledge Management*, **11**(3), 6–15.

Schön, D. (1983). *The Reflective Practitioner*. New York: Basic Books.

Senge, P. (1990). *The Fifth Discipline: The Art and Practice of the Learning Organization*. New York: Doubleday/Currency.

Senge, P., & Scharmer, O. (2001). Community action research: Learning as a community of practitioners, consultants, and researchers, in Reason, P. & Bradbury, H. (Eds.), *Handbook of Action Research, Participatory Inquiry & Practice*. Thousand Oaks, CA: Sage Publications, p. 247.

Shaughnessy, T. W. (1995). Key issue: Achieving peak performance in academic libraries, *Journal of Academic Librarianship* 21(3, May), 155–157.

Somerville, M. M. (2008). Collaborative design and assessment: Learning 'with and for' users. In S. Hiller, et al. (Eds), *Building Effective, Sustainable, Practical Assessment: Proceedings of the Library Assessment Conference*, Seattle, Washington (pp. 337–345). Washington, D.C.: Association of Research Libraries.

Somerville, M. M., & Howard, Z. (2008). Systems thinking: An approach for advancing workplace information literacy. *Australian Library Journal*, 57(2), 257–273.

Somerville, M. M., Howard, Z., & Mirijamdotter, A. (2009). Workplace information literacy: Cultivation strategies for working smarter in 21st Century libraries. In *Pushing the Edge: Explore, Engage, Extend—Proceedings of the 14th Association of College & Research Libraries National Conference*, Seattle, Washington (pp. 119–126), Chicago: Association of College and Research Libraries.

Somerville, M. M., & Yusko, G. (2008). Strategic organizational direction setting: A workplace learning opportunity. In *Reflecting on Successes and Framing Futures—Proceedings of the 5th International Lifelong Learning Conference*, Yeppoon, Australia. Rockhampton, (pp. 366–369), Queensland, Australia: Central Queensland University.

Stacey, R. (2003). Learning as an activity of interdependent people. *The Learning Organization*, 10(6), 325–331.

Stacey, R. D. (2004). *Complex Responsive Processes in Organizations: Learning and Knowledge Creation*. New York, NY: Routledge.

Sullivan, M. (1991). A new leadership paradigm: Empowering library staff and improving performance. *Journal of Library Administration*, 14, 73–85.

Sullivan, M. (2004a). The promise of appreciative inquiry in library organizations. *Library Trends*, 53 (1), 218–229.

Sullivan, M. (2004b). Organizational development in libraries. *Library Administration & Management*, 18 (4), 179–183.

Von Kough, G., Ichijo, K., & Nonaka, I. (2000). *Enabling Knowledge Creation—How to Unlock the Mystery of Tacit Knowledge and Release the Power of Innovation*. New York: Oxford University Press.

Wenger, E. (1998). Communities of practice: learning as a social system. *The Systems Thinker*, 9(5). Available: http://www.co-i-l.com/coil/knowledge-garden/cop/lss.shtml.

Wenger, E. (2000). Communities of practice and social learning systems. *Organization*, 2, 225–246.

Wenger, E. C., & Snyder, W. M. (2000). Communities of practice: The organizational frontier. *Harvard Business Review*, January/February, 139–145.

Wenger, E., McDermott, R., & Snyder, W. (2002). *Cultivating Communities of Practice*. Cambridge, MA: Harvard Business School Press.

Wheatley, M. J. (1994). *Leadership and the New Science: Learning About Organization from an Orderly Universe*. San Francisco, CA: Berrett-Koehler.

Afterword and Acknowledgements

Collaborative information practices encourage workplace inquiry animated by robust information exchange and knowledge creation activities. As consultation circles enlarge, inquiry relationships among people and ideas deepen. When purposeful communication, dialogue, and reflection practices are fortified by enabling organizational structures and systems, workplace culture evolves. Discovery activities, conducted 'with and for' organizational beneficiaries, ensure continuous improvement of user experiences and nimble responsiveness. These conclusions have developed through my interactions with ideas and individuals in workplace settings and professional circles. In the concluding remarks below, I wish to acknowledge particularly significant contributions and contributors.

The groundbreaking work of Christine Bruce and her Australian colleagues guided both organizational change initiatives and grounded theory development. Bruce's work advances the notion that an information encounter, when adequately contextualized, activates and extends prior understanding. This workplace learning study presupposes, therefore, that the genesis of the 'learning' in learning organizations resides in such informing experiences.

Furthermore, Bruce maintains that transferable information finding and using capabilities are best developed concurrent with disciplinary mastery, thereby furthering 'relational', situated information literacy. In the Cal Poly stories, library and information science, knowledge management, computer science, and social informatics content comprised the subject matter with which organizational employees engaged. In explicit inquiry processes, they deepened and broadened their experiences with information.

Concurrently, participants furthered their information practices and information skills through social relationships which expanded their 'intersubjective' connections with colleagues and with ideas, as discovered among fire fighters by another Australian researcher. In addition, visiting Swedish and Australian researchers ensured conversance with international frameworks and intellectual traditions.

This approach to organizational leadership recognizes that individuals 'contain' knowledge. Organizational learning, therefore, depends on enabling individual to access and share information which, when placed in meaningful context, fuels the common understanding that builds collective knowledge capacity. Sustainable large scale learning depends on organizational structures and workplace activities that enable widespread knowledge creation and transfer.

The generation of individual and group capacity requires practice exercising inquiry-based learning processes. Standards endorsed by Australian, European, and North American professional bodies detail information competence capabilities transferable to workplace learning environments. Desirable proficiencies include question formulation and data analysis capabilities which culminate in the identification of organizational 'evidence' to support user-centered decision making and problem solving. At the 'macro' level, these processes also support reconsideration of professional purposes and workplace outcomes. As a consequence, relationships among library colleagues and with campus stakeholders are forever transformed, as are their interactions with information and engagement in inquiry.

These insights benefit from rich professional associations with practitioners and researchers from around the globe, most especially these individuals:

During her three residences at Cal Poly, Swedish social informatics professor Dr. Anita Mirijamdotter infused Scandinavian social democratic traditions into workplace deliberations. Her onsite presence ensured deep egalitarian roots for co-creation of a learning organization, as conceptualized in the 1990's by Peter Senge and others. Mirijamdotter's coaching also nurtured a highly participatory design philosophy which proposed that effective systems are built 'with and for users'. Within the fertile environment of a campus 'learn by doing' educational tradition, a distinctive collaborative design approach developed. It employed user-generated information to produce evidence and advance learning. Mirijamdotter's advice on 'ideal' information systems also influenced the design of workplace communication and decision making systems to optimize sustained interactions with ideas and among colleagues.

This collaborative, information-rich approach to workplace capacity building also benefited from two residencies by Australian researcher Dr. Helen Partridge. She advanced organizational inquiry through introducing both evidence-based information practices and relational information literacy theory. In a complementary fashion, Australian knowledge manager Zaana Howard contributed seasoned insights on enabling and sustaining 'knowledge making' communities of practice within the workplace.

Over the course of this organizational investigation, a distributed research team of university professors invited and analyzed data and information generated by over three hundred students in Australia, Europe, and the United States. Drs. Anita Mirijamdotter and Marita Holst (Sweden); Drs. Erika Rogers, David Gillette, Susan Elrod, and Franz Kurfess (USA); and Dr. Helen Partridge (Australia) supervised the student projects and interpreted their research outcomes. This distributed collegial network continues to provoke and inspire my professional 'sense making' journey.

In addition, as I strived to infuse evolving theory into 'real world' practice, I was aided by enthusiastic and able colleagues. These individuals include librarians Frank Vuotto, Barbara Schader, and Navjit Brar in San Luis Obispo, California; Gordon Yusko, Lydia Collins, Rebecca Feind, and Mary Nino in San José, California; and Cynthia Hashert, Denise Pan, and Marical Farner in Denver, Colorado. Their organizational leadership and project management capabilities opened the doors for workplace innovation.

In addition, Sharon C. Thompson, coordinator of the Librarians for Tomorrow program at the Dr. Martin Luther King, Jr. Library in San José, California, energetically supported production of the numerous presentations and publications out of which this manuscript evolved. Never content to only format content, she unabashedly contributed her insights and observations throughout the manuscript generation process.

With all these colleagues, I share a deep and abiding commitment to discover how to collaboratively create learning communities that elevate collective understanding, enable knowledge creation, and inform organizational responsiveness. To one and all: I am eternally grateful.

Mary M. Somerville
Denver, Colorado, December 15, 2008

Research Papers

Davis, H. L., & Somerville, M. M. (2006). Learning our way to change: Improved institutional alignment. *New Library World, 107*(3/4), 127–140.

Elrod, S., & Somerville, M. M. (2007). Literature based scientific learning: A collaboration model. *Journal of Academic Librarianship, 33*(6), 684–691.

Gillette, D., & Somerville, M. M. (2005). Faculty and student usability and focus group findings inform Digital Teaching Library interface requirements. In *Proceedings of the 12th Annual Syllabus Higher Education Technology Conference*, Los Angeles, California.

Gillette, D. D., & Somerville, M. M.. (2006). Toward lifelong 'knowledge making': Faculty development for student learning in the Cal Poly learning commons. In D. Orr (Ed.), *Lifelong Learning: Partners, Pathways, and Pedagogies: Keynote and Refereed Papers from the 4th International Lifelong Learning Conference*, Yeppoon, Australia, (pp. 117–123). Rockhampton, Queensland, Australia: Central Queensland University.

Howard, Z., & Somerville, M. M. (2008). Building knowledge capabilities: An organisational learning approach. In *Harnessing Knowledge Management to Build Communities—Proceedings of the 11th Annual Conference on Knowledge Management and Intelligent Decision Support* (ACKMIDS08), Ballarat, Victoria, Australia.

Mirijamdotter, M., & Somerville, M. M. (2009). Collaborative design: An SSM-enabled organizational learning approach. *International Journal of Information Technologies and Systems Approach, 2*(1), 48–69.

Mirijamdotter, A., & Somerville, M. M. (2005). Dynamic action inquiry: A systems approach for knowledge based organizational learning. In *Proceedings of the 11th International Conference on Human-Computer Interaction*, Las Vegas, Nevada.

Mirijamdotter, A., & Somerville, M. M. (2008). SSM inspired organizational change in a North American University Library: Lessons learned. In *Public Systems in the Future—Possibilities, Challenges, and Pitfalls: Proceedings of the 31st Information Systems Research Seminar in Scandinavia* (IRIS31), Åre, Sweden.

Mirijamdotter, A., Somerville, M. M., & Holst, M. (2005). An interactive evaluation approach for the creation of collaborative learning commons. In *Proceedings of the 12th European Conference on Information Technology Evaluation (ECITE-12)*, Turku, Finland.

Rogers, E., Somerville, M. M., & Randles, A. (2005). A user-centered content architecture for an academic digital research portal. In P. Kommers & F. Richards (Eds.), *Proceedings of ED-MEDIA 2005—World Conference on Educational Multimedia, Hypermedia, & Telecommunications*, Montreal, Canada, (pp. 1172–1177). Chesapeake, Virginia: Association for the Advancement of Computing in Education.

Somerville, M. M. (2008). Collaborative design and assessment: Learning 'with and for' users. In S. Hiller, et al. (Eds), *Building Effective, Sustainable, Practical Assessment: Proceedings of the Library Assessment Conference*, Seattle, Washington (pp. 337–345). Washington, D.C.: Association of Research Libraries.

Somerville, M. M. (2007). Participatory co-design: A relationship building approach for co-creating libraries of the future. In *Libraries for the Future: Progress, Development and Partnerships—Proceedings of the 73rd International Federation of Library Associations (IFLA) Conference*, Durban, South Africa. Available: http://www.ifla.org/IV/ifla73/papers/122-Somerville-en.pdf

Somerville, M. M., & Brar, N. (2006). Collaborative co-design: The Cal Poly Digital Teaching Library user centric approach. In *Information Access for Global Access: Proceedings of the International Conference on Digital Libraries (ICDL 2006)*, (pp. 175–187). New Delhi, India.

Somerville, M. M., & Brar, N. (2009). A user-centered and evidence-based approach for digital library projects. *The Electronic Library, 27*(3), 409–425

Somerville, M. M., & Brar, N. (2007). Toward co-creation of knowledge in the Interaction Age: An organizational case study. In H. K. Kaul & S. Kaul (Eds.), *Papers of the Tenth National Convention on Knowledge, Library and Information Networking (NACLIN 2007)*, (pp. 367–376). New Delhi, India: Developing Library Network.

Somerville, M. M., & Collins, L. (2008). Collaborative design: A learner-centered library planning approach. *The Electronic Library, 26*(6), 803–820.

Somerville, M. M., & Howard, Z. (2008). Systems thinking: An approach for advancing workplace information literacy. *Australian Library Journal, 57*(2), 257–273.

Somerville, M. M., Howard, Z., & Mirijamdotter, A. (2009). Workplace information literacy: Cultivation strategies for working smarter in 21st Century libraries. In *Pushing the Edge: Explore, Engage, Extend—Proceedings of the 14th Association of College & Research Libraries National Conference*, Seattle, Washington, (pp. 119–126), Chicago: Association of College and Research Libraries.

Somerville, M. M., Huston, M. E., & Mirijamdotter, A. (2005). Building on what we know: Staff development in the digital age. *The Electronic Library, 23*(4), 480–491.

Somerville, M. M., & Mirijamdotter, A. (2005). Working smarter: An applied model for "better thinking" in dynamic information organizations. In *Currents and convergence—Navigating the rivers of change: Proceedings of the 12th National Conference of the Association of College and Research Libraries (ACRL)*, Minneapolis, Minnesota, (pp. 103–111). Chicago: Association of College and Research Libraries.

Somerville, M. M., Mirijamdotter, A., & Collins, L. (2006). Systems thinking and information literacy: Elements of a knowledge enabling workplace environment. In *Proceedings of the 39th Annual Hawaii International Conference on Systems Sciences*

(*HICSS-39*), Koloa, Kauai. Los Alamitos, California: IEEE Computer Society.

Somerville, M. M., & Nino, M. (2007). Collaborative co-design: A user-centric approach for advancement of organizational learning. *Performance Measurement and Metrics: The International Journal for Library and Information Services, 8*(3), 180–188.

Somerville, M. M., Rogers, E., Mirijamdotter, A., & Partridge, H. (2007). Collaborative evidence-based information practice: The Cal Poly digital learning initiative. In E. Connor (Ed.), *Evidence-Based Librarianship: Case Studies and Active Learning Exercises* (pp. 141–161). Oxford, England: Chandos Publishing.

Somerville, M. M., Schader, B., & Huston, M. E. (2005). Rethinking what we do and how we do it: Systems thinking strategies for library leadership. *Australian Academic and Research Libraries 36*(4), 214–227.

Somerville, M. M., & Vazquez, F. (2004). Constructivist workplace learning: An idealized design project. In P. A. Danaher, C. Macpherson, F. Nouwens, & D. Orr (Eds.), *Proceedings of the 3rd International Lifelong Learning Conference*, Yeppoon, Queensland, Australia, (pp. 300–305 plus errata page). Rockhampton, Australia: Central Queensland University.

Somerville, M. M., & Vuotto, F. (2005). If you build it with them, they will come: Digital research portal design and development strategies. *Internet Reference Services Quarterly: A Journal of Innovative Information Practice, Technologies, and Resources 10*(1), 77–94.

Somerville, M. M., & Yusko, G. (2008). Strategic organizational direction setting: A workplace learning opportunity. In *Reflecting on Successes and Framing Futures—Proceedings of the 5th International Lifelong Learning Conference*, Yeppoon, Australia. Rockhampton, (pp. 366–369), Queensland, Australia: Central Queensland University.